the find

the
find

The Housing Works Book of Decorating
with Thrift Shop Treasures, Flea Market
Objects, and Vintage Details

Stan Williams

Foreword by Charles King,
founder of Housing Works
Photographs by Jim Franco

Clarkson Potter/Publishers
New York

Library of Congress Cataloging-in-Publication Data
Williams, Stan.
The find / Stan Williams.—1st ed.
1. Antiques in interior decoration.   I. Title.
NK2115.5.A5W55   2009
747—dc22   2008038471

ISBN 978-0-307-40625-5

Printed in China

Design by Lauren Monchik

Principal photography by Jim Franco
Additional photographs by Bob Greenspan: pages 4 (bottom); 6 (middle row, left and right;
bottom row, right); 28; 31 (left); 40; 42–43; 45 (bottom); 46–48; 51–71; 81; 94–99; 130;
144–147; 156–157; 186; 204–217; 240.
Photograph by Anna Moller: page 10.

10 9 8 7 6 5 4 3 2 1

First Edition

dedication

To Mom—who showed my sister and me how to pour and paint candles; sew simple pillows, tablecloths, place mats, and curtains; create sparkly Christmas ornaments out of beads, bows, and Styrofoam; and embroider flowers on scraps of fabric—and to Dad—who proved to me that with a bit of elbow grease, a swipe of sandpaper, and a fresh coat of paint, stain, or varnish, the most desperate piece of furniture can look even better than brand-new

contents

foreword

Upscale charity thrift shops are now relatively commonplace,
but when Housing Works opened its first thrift shop in
1995, nobody, including me, thought the concept would work
(our landlord didn't think so, either; he would give us only
a short-term lease). We broke even on our initial $150,000
investment in less than six months. Twelve years later we have
seven Housing Works Thrift Shops that earn $10 million a year
for homeless and low-income people living with HIV/AIDS.

ABOVE New York City's original Housing Works Thrift Shop on West 17th Street.

OPPOSITE Keep an open mind to ponder the imaginative uses for vintage and thrift-store finds like this jumble of rusty skeleton keys.

The Housing Works Thrift Shops brilliantly marry New Yorkers' self-serving and selfless impulses (let's face it: we all have both). On the one hand, our customers find incredible bargains on high-end and one-of-a-kind clothing and home furnishings; on the other, every dollar they spend and every item they donate goes to a proverbial "good cause." It doesn't hurt that our stores are cheerful and stylishly organized and have an ambiance one finds only when people come together to help others. Our employees and customers are lit from within.

The clever yoking of bargain hunting with charity is only half the story of the Housing Works Thrift Shops. The other half is the hundreds of homeless and low-income men and women who have gone through our Second Life Job Training program and obtained jobs at the Thrift Shops and other Housing Works businesses. No matter how many times I walk into one of our locations, I am moved by the sight of formerly homeless and ill folks now proudly doing their jobs.

Thrifts allow Housing Works to pursue its lofty but achievable mission: to end the AIDS epidemic in the United States and abroad and to provide access to care and treatment for everyone living with the disease. For a decade now, the world has possessed the prevention and treatment tools necessary to achieve these goals, but 2 million people per year die of a preventable illness that has already claimed 25 million lives.

This book is all about how talented people use vintage objects to create beautiful spaces. I don't think that the connection between the kind of beauty they are able to create and places like Housing Works Thrift Shops is coincidental. Vintage furnishings provide us with a link to past eras and past lives—in essence, to one another. So does shopping, donating, or volunteering at an organization like Housing Works. When the two go together, it's magic.

Now get out there and shop!

Charles King
President and CEO, Housing Works

introduction

the adventure starts

I credit none other than the good old American garage sale with opening my eyes to the excitement of finding treasures in someone else's castoffs. Furniture lining driveways just begging for a new coat of paint or fresh drawer pulls, plates and bowls still alive with color and style, funny framed prints, empty picture frames, futuristic easy chairs, Mediterranean dinettes, and the list goes on. It's not so much that I had the desire to own each and every one of these items. In fact, I wasn't always attracted to all I stumbled upon. But it was the thrill of touching and experiencing these used goods that never failed to evoke warm memories or charge my imagination.

I grew up in Independence, Missouri, and the Kansas City suburb was a buzzing hotbed of shopping during the mid-'70s. Neighborhood women who lived on streets with names like Ponca and Cheyenne had spent the previous year stashing away all of their castoffs, just waiting for one of those sunny summer days to have a garage sale.

During the week leading up to the big event, these at-home shop-keepers would spend hours tearing off shards of masking tape to serve as price tags for their metal Tonka toy trucks and their everything-in-this-box-for-$1 hodgepodge. They would arrange their offerings on rickety card tables (sometimes the stray redwood picnic table, definitely *not* for sale!) and hoist up the doors of their single-car garages for shoppers who were already cruising the streets at 7 a.m. ready to snap up a good deal.

My aunt Diana was usually among those early birds who hovered in the first shift. She managed her summer Thursday thrifting adventures on Wednesday nights by reading all the garage sale listings in the Independence *Examiner*. She and my mother would lay out detailed plans for the coming day, circling, marking, and checking off all the good-looking sales in their respective papers. They would plot their path, street by street, so come garage-sale time, they wouldn't miss a single advertised "ton of baby clothes" or "brand-new bedroom set."

ABOVE LEFT Black frames unify a grouping of graphic artwork.

ABOVE CENTER Even butterflies, moths, and bugs preserved under glass transform into decorative elements in hardware sculptor Carl Martinez's kitchen.

ABOVE RIGHT For a manly accent to their foyer, designer John Bartlett and framer John Esty hung a pair of tattered boxing gloves on the pegs of a rustic wood harrow once used for planting seeds.

OPPOSITE Flea markets can be a dis-covery ground for everything from fine antiques to heartwarming collectables.

PREVIOUS PAGES China cups and useful dishes are examples of the kinds of treasures found at thrift stores, flea markets, and garage sales.

ABOVE Wood dining chairs heaped high to the ceiling are an everyday find in thrift shops like Housing Works.

OPPOSITE Fine-tune your peripheral vision to zero in on fascinating decorative elements, such as this curtained Victorian birdcage discovered at a flea market.

These shopping extravaganzas usually took place on clear days when school was out. (Back then where I grew up, garage sales only took place in the summer and almost never on a weekend.) My mother; my sister, Cheryl; Diana; and her kids would pack our Chevy Impala on our mission to find everything from board games to cutting knives. When relatives were up from Southern Missouri, the gang would have to separate into two cars to hold all the thrift seekers along with their newly found garage goodies.

We scoured musty, dark garages for puzzles that still had all their pieces or a set of dishes that were unchipped and actually matched. We might then head over to a long, winding driveway that was packed on either side with everything from handmade, crocheted doilies and quilt squares to perfectly good home appliances and porcelain dogs for Cheryl's collection. Once the goods were fully examined, and the coinage rendered, we headed off to the next location on our quickly shortening list. That's not to say that there were no detours along the way. Mom might ease the car slowly past what was clearly an overstapled and thumbtacked telephone pole that held the promise of a cardboard sign announcing a multifamily sale right around the corner. Diana would squeal with delight at the surprise of an additional stop and jot down the address as fast as we could read it back to her.

A few years later as a university student, I coerced my dad into helping me drag home a huge, oak teacher's desk that I promised I would refinish for my bedroom. I think I paid $10 for it back in 1984. My dad, an elementary school principal at the time, wasn't too pleased. "If I'd known you wanted a teacher's desk, I could have probably found you one for free," I remember his saying. And despite my vow to make the desk look new again, and Dad's displeasure with the brown chunk of wood sitting in the middle of his garage, he ended up refinishing it for me. Its surface shined with new coats of stain and varnish, and the rough edges of the drawers were lovingly smoothed with careful swipes of sandpaper.

I think of this desk every time I write at the wobbly-legged dining room table I bought on the street for $75, including delivery. The table's

ABOVE LEFT Hung low over a dining room table, dangled above a desk in a home office, or even suspended from the ceiling in a bathroom, this graceful Victorian luster is a true find.

ABOVE RIGHT Financial advisor and collector Alvin Hall with a Danish modern chair he found one evening while nightclubbing in New York City's East Village.

history with me dates back to the early '90s, when I bought it from a crusty old woman who used to drive her dilapidated, graffiti-riddled van into Manhattan from New Jersey, fresh off a trek of estate sales in the suburbs; every Sunday she set up shop on a pedestrian mall on lower Sixth Avenue. I do love this table with its intricate inlaid wooden top and metal-ring leg ornaments, but it certainly doesn't take the place of my big old sturdy desk that now lives with my sister back in the Midwest.

I could easily replace my dining room table with one that doesn't jiggle when a guest starts cutting into a juicy steak or creak and moan when I'm sitting there paying the bills, but I can't part with that temperamental table. I'm attached to it, just like I adored my beloved desk. Both are beautiful—scuffs, dings, and all. When I run my fingers along the old desk's surface, I can literally feel the imprint of that term paper I wrote about an obscure French poet. Along the top edge of the desk drawer that used to lock, there's a splintery, ominous scar, evidence that someone in its history must have kept inside a top-secret grade book or a treasure trove of Coke change, and had lost the key. Like that utilitarian

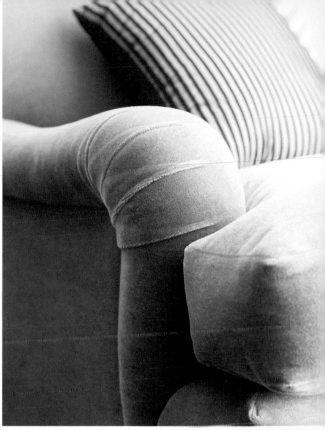

desk, my dining room table has had a pretty impressive life under my care. It has been the centerpiece of memorable parties where its scrapes and scratches have been cloaked in a stunning red-and-white floral-print tablecloth from the 1960s that I found in a thrift shop in Independence. Since my New York apartment is small by most people's standards, the table has conveniently doubled as a work space where I've written magazine articles, iced cupcakes, and glued snowflakes on handmade Christmas cards.

unleashing imagination

Decorating with thrift home furnishings is an exercise in shopping with an open mind and bringing the past fast-forward into the present. What I used to think of as other people's old stuff sitting out in the driveway or piled high in a junk store (or *junque,* if the shopkeeper was trying to make it sound fancy) is now referred to as *vintage.* No longer is there any stigma attached to buying someone else's castoffs. Thanks to invitingly

ABOVE LEFT Interior designer Randall Beale took a collection of dissimilar objects—a Maxim Velcovsky boot for Studio Qubus, a model of a Meji giant prawn from Nina Griscom, a corked pig by Harry Allen for Area-ware, and a branch of coral—and made their white quality work together for picture perfect results.

ABOVE RIGHT Upholstered furniture in all shapes and sizes arrives on a daily basis to thrift stores across the country.

BELOW LEFT Prop stylist Joe Maer took flea-market china—some made in England, others in Japan—and unified them into a sophisticated, one-of-a-kind, blue-and-white-themed tea party.

BELOW RIGHT Who says you have to have all new appliances? If you're Heather Chadduck, an old one will do, especially if it's the Chambers stove she's always dreamed of owning. She bought two stoves on eBay and combined the best parts from each to assemble a complete working one.

merchandised thrift stores like Housing Works in New York City and Web sites like eBay and Craigslist, used goods are getting a new life, and are finding themselves an integral part of expressing personal style through decorating.

Rather than spend my time shopping for "real" antiques in established shops, I'd much rather slather on the sunblock and spend a day with my fabulous decorator friend Mark Ciolli digging through precarious-looking pieces of lighting fixtures and boxes of sea coral (oh, and quite a bit of trash, too!) at a drive-in theater swap meet in Fort Lauderdale. When I'm not perusing wares at Housing Works, I'll hop the A train to Harlem to poke around in Lisa Bethelmy's 400-square-foot nook called Finderz Keeperz Vintage Boutique. You know you're in for

an adventure when you walk by the hole-in-the-wall, which is announced by a packed rack of old clothes hanging out front next to a metal fold-up table almost always strewn with an array of brightly colored plates, whimsically patterned drinking vessels, and the occasional collectable glass vase. When you spy a treasure stashed away in a cluttered corner of Lisa's shop and make a grab for it, you never know what will fall from out of nowhere, which more often than not results in an additional purchase. (I was once surprised by a duo of paint-by-number landscapes in pale wood frames from the 1960s, perfect for my photographer friend Bob Greenspan's budding collection.)

The true beauty of buying thrift, according to Maxwell Gillingham-Ryan, founder of the *Apartment Therapy* Web sites, is that when you buy a used piece of furniture, it already has lived a life, has a history, and is

ABOVE LEFT Vintage necklaces and golden lockets need not always be worn around the neck. Chadduck tapped into her imagination for a sparkling display in her bedroom that also keeps her favorite jewelry close at hand.

probably of better quality than something new at the same price. "It's like buying jeans," he says. "You never really want a new pair of jeans. What you really want is a pair that already has a life." There is nothing wrong with tiptoeing around a stately Biedermeier credenza or oohing and aahing over a rare, ebonized Napoléon III secretary in an established antiques store. For many people, it can be an entirely satisfying and creative shopping moment. I admire those upscale antiques shops for their cultivated tastes, their crème de la crème of furniture, and their discerning and loyal clientele. Even so, I prefer an element of surprise discovering what dwells beneath a pile of hand-embroidered napkins or at the bottom of a box overflowing with old "Hints from Heloise" day planners, reams of sheet music, maps from around the world, or amusement park guides. Thrift shops, flea markets, and garage sales hold so much more intrigue for me, since I am always entertained by their guarantee of complete surprise.

moving merchandise

Exchange of merchandise occurs in thrift stores all over the country as empty nesters sell the big house and relocate to smaller quarters. Rooms are emptied as a whole new décor is established, or former residents move out to make room for the next. Remember, these thrift stores run just like other retailers: they absolutely have to make the cash register ring. If a piece of merchandise, especially something like a large sofa or a grandiose armoire, sits on the floor a day too long, its price will soon be slashed to make room for an incoming donation. This means that you're not going to pay antiques-store prices for a fabulous 1960s chrome coffee table or a nineteenth-century full-lead mirror.

Blanche Hansma, who has overseen donations at Housing Works for more than a decade, has witnessed her share of major decorating steals take place on the sales floor, even though she assigns fair prices to donated goods. "I went crazy one day when I found out that the store had two Jonathan Adler lamps at $75 a piece, when I would have priced them at $150 a piece. But since the lamps had no identifying markings

ABOVE Common mix-and-match silverware found at thrift stores, flea markets, and garage sales adds a time-honored quality to an elegant table or even to an everyday place setting.

OPPOSITE Repurposing an object beyond its intended use is certain to create a conversation piece. Designer John Derian used a much-stomped-upon vintage infield base to warm the seat of a painted flea-market chair.

MAKE A THRIFT-SHOPPING KIT
YOUR DESIGN KIT IS REALLY JUST A WAY OF
PREPARING FOR THRIFT-SHOPPING PURSUITS.

When the urge to go thrift-shopping hits, you'll have the tools ready to help you organize your search, and to be prepared to buy when you run across that must-have item. In your shopping kit, include the following:

- A good tape measure. Invest in one that measures 8 to 10 feet, stretches out and closes with ease, and is convenient to carry.

- A camera. A digital photograph, even if on your mobile phone, allows you the luxury of sending off the image to an expert, a friend, or even your own decorator for a bit of advice before you make the purchase.

- Dry dust wipes, such as a Swiffer, which just might remove years of grime to reveal a furniture treasure.

- A design notebook. Fill it with budgets, wish lists, photos of design inspiration, essential measurements, fabric swatches, and important phone numbers for shipping and delivery. Keep referring to your design notebook, and stick with the items you feel you absolutely need and those that fit in your budget. The best thing about a design notebook is that you will always know where you slowed down in your shopping pursuits. Then once you're in the shopping mood again, just pick up where you left off.

on them, they went out the door as a bargain. People say to me all the time, 'Don't feel bad when something slips through. It's supposed to be that way. It's a thrift store.'"

The rapid rate at which products arrive and exit a thrift store should always keep you on your toes for that rare moment you set sight on, say, a midcentury desk at a price that suits your budget or a coppery metal 1960s cake carrier you've always wanted. Act fast and buy it, or someone else will. The benefit to you, the consumer, is that you can find unique items at a fraction of the original price. Why go to a furniture chain store and spend $5,000 on a phony antique chest of drawers when you can get the real thing for less than $750?

Decorators know that thrift stores, flea markets, and garage sales are perfect places to find inexpensive goods that with a little TLC can be resold to their clients at hefty markups. The most creative and successful decorators make it a point to stop by their favorite thrift stores at least once a week. Before opening time on any given day at Housing Works, expect to see decorators, clip-boards and client folders in hand, eagerly waiting for those doors to be unlocked so they can get first crack at the best selection of merchandise. These pros have been hired by clients to inject an individualized style into their homes. Thrift stores easily satisfy their need to add a sense of history and permanence to a room that may be void of personal flair.

scratching the surface

Before you head out on a thrifty scavenger hunt, take a loose inventory of what you already own and form some ideas of what you would like to find. It's almost like going to the grocery store; you would never buy a gallon of milk if you already had two sitting in the fridge. At the same time, don't give up on the Shaker bed frame you've had your heart set on since you started living on your own if it doesn't appear out of thin air. Instead, savor the thrift-shop experience. When you're shopping with the direct intention of buying, you are not a failure if you walk out the door empty-handed. Allow your thrift shopping to take you on a journey through time where your imagination wanders over each and every object that strikes your fancy—even if it's just for a fleeting moment. Who tatted the lace on that butterfly-embroidered table runner? What front porch did that metal glider once call home? How did that woodworker get the corners of that drawer mitered so perfectly without a single nail? Simply put, enjoy the moment and put off buying something for another visit.

treasures will appear

Always have your peripheral vision set to reveal the unexpected. Once while I was way too focused on digging through a cubby of old magazines from the 1960s in a thrift store in Waxhaw, North Carolina, I somehow had my peripheral vision turned off, completely overlooking a signed print of the entire cast of the movie *Nine to Five*. Thankfully, my eagle-eyed partner, Veli, saw it, snapped it up, and sneaked it back to New York to become one of my most prized

ABOVE French funereal vases found at a flea market get a new life next to a vintage demijohn on Heather Chadduck's mantel.

Real Simple's Kristin van Ogtrop at Housing Works.

TOP SHOPPER: Thrift Tips from *Real Simple*'s Kristin van Ogtrop

You can't walk around any room in my house without bumping into something I bought at a thrift store, a garage sale, or a consignment store. (Or, even better, got for free on the curb because someone else was throwing it out, hence the cool three-legged metal chair that sits on my front porch.) I've never had a problem reclaiming items that someone else no longer loved, with the possible exception of the gorgeous peach silk nightgown I bought at a thrift store on the Upper West Side of Manhattan in the '80s that never did quite manage to smell new again. Now that I am a homeowner, there is a particular consignment store I visit in Greenwich, Connecticut, that never disappoints, even if half the time I come home with an item (okay, multiple items) quite different from what I set out to find. Which leads me to my rules for thrift-store furniture shopping:

- Keep an open mind. If what you're looking for is an end table but what you fall in love with is a bongo drum, ask yourself this: Can A become B? In the case of the bongo drum as end table, the answer is yes.
- These two words should be like tickertape looping through your mind as you're looking at vintage furniture: PAINT, FABRIC. PAINT, FABRIC. These facets of an item are easy to change relatively inexpensively, and can instantly turn a sow's ear into a silk purse. Just ask me about the chair with the mottled caning and really ugly seat that my sister once bought in Delaware for $35 that I wish I had grabbed before she saw it. She spray painted the caning and frame black and changed the fabric, and now it sits proudly in her living room (and makes me a little bit mad every time I walk by it).
- If you love something and are astounded by how cheap it is but don't know where it will go, buy it. You will probably find a place for it, and even if you don't, giving it away to someone else won't cost you that much. And you'll be rewarded with good karma.
- Alternatively, resist the siren song of the bargain. If you are tempted to buy something because it is so inexpensive—but not because you love it—back away. You need to surround yourself with things you love, whether they cost $2 or $2,000. Anything else is just junk.
- Never leave the house without a tape measure, even if it makes your bag heavier. And if you can manage it, having someone at home whom you can call from the store to do emergency measuring of a certain area of your house can come in handy. Just ask my husband about the "Living Room Coffee Table Incident." I was out and about and saw what may have been the elusive perfect table. He wasn't home to measure the space for me, and when I returned to the store the following Saturday, it was gone. Sigh. Which leads me to . . .
- If you see something you really want to buy, don't hesitate: pick it up, sit on it, and cover the item with your entire body if you have to. If you don't believe me, ask my mother about the green garden bench at an antiques show in Massachusetts. It was metal and a bit rusty but the perfect size for her back deck, which overlooks the lovely side garden. Just imagine: coffee in the morning, drinks in the afternoon, all on the perfectly proportioned bench, which had sold when we returned to the vendor two hours later. Now it's been more than a year, and I don't think either of us has recovered.

Christmas gifts. Had I noticed this print, I would have bought it without hesitation, knowing that it would perfectly accent the other black-and-white photographs I have displayed along the stairs that lead up to my living room.

Remain open to treasures that'll suddenly seem to appear all over or that might not be glaring right in front of you. Reach beyond first impressions and uncover that metal cafeteria stool hidden under a pile of old record albums. Or what about that ugly-looking desk with ghastly pulls? Would a good scrubbing, a fresh coat of glossy paint, and shiny new knobs make it completely serviceable and attractive in your home office? If you take a metal brush to that rusty outdoor furniture, as Heather Chadduck, *Cottage Living*'s style director, recommends, will you discover that with a little paint, something that's secondhand doesn't have to be second-rate?

Your own living situation will help determine many factors of just how much used furniture or accessories you can actually absorb. Before you head out, study and revise your list, separating everything you need for comfort and everything you want for decoration, and keep it with you at all times. Remember, when you see an item on your list, be ready to buy it. The item most likely won't be there when you finally decide next week that you've got to have it. Evaluate your living space, as each person's experience is unique. If you are moving into your very first apartment, then you probably need almost everything. Hardwood furniture, useful sets of dishes, and possibly a colorful lamp might be on your shopping list. On the other hand, if you are relocating to your second, third, or fourth home, you might already have a lot of furnishings you wish to continue using. Adding some bedroom furniture, a side chair, or just some freshened-up accessories and accent pieces might help complete your new décor.

a balancing act

Striking a balance between what is new and what is thrift is key when starting to decorate. Gillingham-Ryan recommends a workable

ABOVE John Derian turned a wood mat into a sort of bulletin board where he displays special photos, postcards, phone numbers, and anything else that inspires him.

OPPOSITE Quality furniture no longer available at regular retail stores, like the bentwood sofa and chairs in Peter Moruzzi and Lauren LeBaron's LA rumpus room, is still plentiful at thrift shops and flea markets.

50 percent rule (half thrift, half new) as a good one to follow. Unless you are extremely confident in your thrift abilities, fashion your home much like you would your wardrobe. Most people really don't want to wear only old clothes or shop for just one brand. When you have variety in a wardrobe, the old and the new tend to accent each other, achieving a style attributable to you and only you, much in the same way you would decorate. I love the '50s-style server that I bought from the same vendor who sold me my dining room table just as much as the striped hand-tufted rug Gene Meyer designed for my living room and the aubergine sofa I bought at Crate & Barrel.

As with any decorating scheme, whether it's incorporating the previously owned or the brand-spanking-new, select only items that truly make you happy, and never anything that just says "so-so." Focus on items that send a message to your soul, jog an endearing sentiment, or evoke a cherished memory. That way, it'll be easier to digest the gigantic amount of merchandise that shows up in a thrift store, is set out at a

ABOVE LEFT Garage sales, like the annual event held by LA's Ruth Handel and Johanna Wendt, turn up decorative accents sure to prompt a grin.

ABOVE RIGHT Flea-market furniture can trigger creative uses to resolve unusual storage situations. At Maison Rêve near San Francisco, Yasmine McGrane created a place to stash fireplace logs in an old pie safe.

OPPOSITE The beauty of buying vintage furniture is that it comes with a past life. A shiny new piece doesn't hold the same design impact as this simple dressing table in the serene surroundings of a beach cottage on Fire Island.

The centerpiece of Heather Chadduck's living room is a fireplace she fashioned out of oyster shells she procured from a local restaurant. Before delivering them to her home, the restaurant thoroughly scoured them in its industrial dishwasher. To further safeguard against sea odors, Chadduck let the shells bask in the sunshine for several days before bringing them indoors and starting her project. "It was like a big puzzle putting all those pieces together, and I love it."

swap meet, or pops up at an online selling site, since it's impossible to love everything. If you just "kind of" like that romatic velvet tuxedo sofa or "sort of" want that orange piece of Hall pottery even though its color repulses you, then these items are not for you. They might represent a trusted heritage or exude incredible style, but they're probably better off in someone else's home. Edit in your mind. Love it in your heart.

Whether it's illustrated by flea-market finds in San Francisco or thrift-store triumphs in New York, this book will begin training your eye to focus on top-quality products that will complement the style in which you live. "Find your style, and stay true to the things you truly love, and it will all come together," says Chadduck. As with anything, decorating with thrift just takes a little time and patience as you discover your own look. If you feel you have to attach a pedigree to feel better decorating with a bunch of used stuff, then call it vintage. Or if it makes you feel more confident buying old things, call them antiques, even though the term is loosely applied to products that are at least a hundred years old. Either way, it's all about learning how to discover the unusual in the mundane, the useful in the slightly run-down, and the beauty that might be exposed with the swipe of a damp cotton cloth or a lovingly applied fresh coat of paint.

planning makes perfect

As you head out to the local thrift stores, flea markets, and garage sales, give serious thought to how you want your finished environment to look and how you will achieve it. Some people like rules, but really, almost anything goes, as long as it looks planned and you absolutely love it. Thumb through magazines and tear out pages that appeal to you. Note how different wood tones look when put together and how fabric patterns mix and match. Assess the way furniture is placed and evaluate the practical flow of a room. Think about how you are going to use each room.

If you're starting out with a fresh decorating palette, is there one furniture item, like a bed or a dining table, that'll be the main useful element of the room? If it makes it easier for you, why not set a theme?

Are you drawn to the rich hues of dark woods and deep-colored upholstery of an old English library? Or do you prefer midcentury starkness and subdued patterns void of color? Do you like to express yourself with lots of hanging art and collected vignettes of favorite items? If you can establish flexible parameters for setting your style, they'll help focus your ultimate decorating goals. And then there's the money factor. Gillingham-Ryan stresses that when shopping for thrift, it's important to make sure those new-old purchases fit within an already-set budget. With prices that are low and financially attractive, the unusual and heart-tugging offerings can lead to impulse buys that end up contributing to unwanted clutter.

When creating a new living environment, Gillingham-Ryan recommends getting rid of as much of the old stuff as you can bear. Thoroughly declutter your house so that you have room to decorate with ease. "When you hold on to too many old things," he says, "your mind is not open to bringing in the new."

collect your thoughts

Once you feel fully inspired to start buying furniture, have sketched out rough ideas of how you want your space to look, and have set your budget, make sure that any treasure you stumble upon will actually fit into the space for which it is intended. Will it fit through the door? Up the elevator? Into its designated place? And how do you think you're going to get a large item home? Can you get it into a taxi or can you ring up a really good friend with a big car to lend you a hand? Just like the decorators who shop in thrift stores, research delivery services you can call at the last minute to come out, load up your purchase, and take it right to your door. Thrift stores like Housing Works will sometimes hold a piece of merchandise until the end of the day, but if you leave it there too long, it's destined to be off to the next willing shopper.

Alvin Hall, a financial advisor and avid collector of art and photography, recalls an evening of nightclubbing that endured into the wee hours of the morning in New York's East Village where he had to

ABOVE The wall sconce in her breakfast nook adds a romantic detail against the grooved wall that Chadduck had installed.

OPPOSITE To create a room that exudes texture, color, and a dash of humor, interior designer Randall Beale mixed vintage discoveries and fine antiques with treasured art acquisitions.

negotiate both the financial and the logistical factors of a surprising street find. On his way home, Hall stumbled upon a pair of modernist wood chairs sitting on the sidewalk in front of a little thrift store. Despite the meager amount of cash in his wallet, he brokered a $50 deal for the set, but that was all the money he had. He absolutely had to have those chairs, so instead of hailing a taxi to take him more than twenty blocks, he decided to hoof it home with his chairs in hand. Thanks to a little persistence, not to mention strong arms and legs, Hall has two beautiful chairs that he still uses at his breakfast table. What's more, even though Hall had no idea of the real value of his pieces (he still isn't sure, as the chairs possess no overt markings), he went with his gut to buy something he most certainly loved and he didn't blow his budget!

Just as Hall ventured bravely into buying something he adored from a stranger in the street, you, too, will banish your decorating fears and prove that you don't have to be a Sotheby's appraiser to spot a good piece of furniture, one useful and packed with design integrity. You're not necessarily looking for investment pieces; you're on the hunt for functional items that will accent your home as well as mix right in with the items you may already own.

Get a leap on your prep work (other than having enough cash on you!) by starting a design kit, packed with everything you need to make an educated thrift purchase (see page 24). A design kit will help you focus on your functional needs, stay within a budget, and enforce a design concept. Refer to it when you need to feel inspired, confident, or creative. That way you can act fast when you find that piece you've just got to have. If you snooze, you lose.

proceed fearlessly

The biggest mistake made in any home-decorating project is being afraid to make a mistake. Relax. Practically any goof you're likely to make is easily corrected. Let's say that one day you wake up and think, "I'm going to paint that wall a bright tangerine." So you go out to the paint shop, buy a nice can of the citrus hue, and paint the wall. But then you decide that you absolutely hate it. No problem. Just buy a different color of paint and redo the wall. Think of thrift shopping in the same way. If you've bought a piece of furniture at a charity thrift shop that you can't live with, or can't seem to figure out how to repair or refinish, just donate it right back to the store and take the tax deduction, or sell it to someone else.

Try giving yourself a couple of days before you decide to banish a thrifty find from your home. Remember why you fell in love with it in the first place. Move it from room to room. See where it might sit best. Can you give it a coat of paint that will make it fit in with the rest of your décor? Or can you find an unexpected use for it that might just add interest to your home? Who says you can't use a large desk as a breakfast table or a wood chair as a side table? There's a reason you decided you had to have it, so maybe looking at it in a different light will rekindle its appeal. But if you cannot find the love, then it's time to get rid of it.

the gift of thrift

On one crisp autumn afternoon, my friend Sharleen Reeder displayed a trio of Homer Laughlin's Marigold china on an old server in the front of her shop, Luticia Clementine's in Independence, Missouri. I am not a china aficionado, but I couldn't pull my attention away from these delicate plates from the 1930s. Featuring a colonial couple in black silhouette—she all pretty in pink with a matching unfurled fan, he curtseying in a ruffled shirt and pale blue knee britches—these pieces tell a tale of whimsy and romance. At the same time, they projected a sense of mystery around their graceful and stately characters, especially since their black faces were void of detail yet their clothes and accessories were in beautiful pastel hues.

I reached for these treasures and without flipping them over to check their stamps, carried them up to Reeder's register, where she meticulously wrapped them in red, pink, and blue tissue and carefully stacked them in one of her signature black-and-white polka-dotted bags. As she passed me my change, Reeder paused: "I'm so happy you bought these," she said to me as her bright blue eyes sparkled. "I can tell you love them

ABOVE A turn-of-the-century egg basket becomes a home for Alvin Hall's beloved collection of silver African rings.

OPPOSITE Sometimes all it takes is a new color scheme to change a piece of furniture's attitude. A set of metal twin beds at a beach house, when dressed up in pretty pink sheets, still look up-to-date and inviting.

just as much as I do." She zeroed in on a sentiment we both shared when we made our separate discoveries. Still, I had absolutely no idea as to how I was going to integrate those lovely plates into my apartment.

Back to New York these china plates flew, all wrapped carefully in my carry-on bags. Once I got them home, I laid them out on that wiggly dining room table, where I moved them around for a few weeks. I daydreamed about serving spiced cookies or coconut cupcakes on them, and showed them off to guests, who marveled at the mystifying couple they represented. And as much as I knew I possessed something truly unique and special, I also realized that their permanent home was not with me. Then came the birthday of my amazing, va-va-va-voom pal Beverly "Bevy" Smith, a New York style writer and television personality. It was during her birthday week that it struck me; these plates were destined for her Harlem home. During an intimate dinner of close friends who showered her with gorgeous gifts, I have to admit, I became a little reluctant to offer the plates I had bought used for $12. A gorgeous scented candle went by; a fascinating art book was heralded; a luxurious gift certificate presented. I was up next. As Smith started peeling back the tissue paper around the plates, my brain was a nervous wreck, but my heart kept telling me she would love those plates as much as I did. As the wrappings fell off, an art connoisseur at the table shrieked, "Is that a Kara Walker?" It just happened that the artist Kara Walker was showing a retrospective of her work depicting American race relations executed in black-and-white silhouette at the Whitney. I revealed that I was unfamiliar with the artist, but as the plates were passed around the table for all to admire, I was just as comforted as Reeder was when a treasure she had fallen head over heels for was going to a warm, welcoming home.

furniture

love it or leave it

While the bargain factor of used furniture rates high, decorators and home enthusiasts across the country prize thrift shops as an indispensable resource. Unique finds, such as turn-of-the-century armchairs, 1930s dressing tables, and Swedish modern credenzas can simply not be found in traditional furniture stores. With a touch of ingenuity, some sanding, and a dab of fresh paint, a discarded chair stands out as a dining room showpiece, a down-and-out dresser prevails as a regal storage solution, and a rusty metal table transforms into a balcony centerpiece. At thrift shops you'll see a revolving assortment of antiques, junk-shop bric-a-brac, flea-market finds, and everyday, useful home goods.

Professional decorators and furniture boutique owners regularly scour thrift stores and flea markets for merchandise. They look beyond the replaceable ugly knobs on a cabinet, or notice the decorative wood bases and scrolls on a nonworking Victorian piano that could be repurposed to accentuate another design project. One steamy summer afternoon I went to Housing Works with decorator Mark Ciolli, principal of Carl & Co. On that specific shopping trip, I witnessed a furniture transaction that happened so quickly and smugly that it felt like I was on some kind of secret mission and the detective had found his subject hiding under a pile of junk in a store. In a sense, he had. Yes, I saw the glass-topped table priced at $45. Oh yeah, it was the one that had two metal dinette chairs by it and a pile of Mediterranean-style accent pillows on it. The glass was thin and poorly cut, and I couldn't understand why Ciolli would get so worked up over what looked like garbage to me. I leaned against an upended tacky, ruffled floral sofa as he flipped open his mobile phone and started dictating specific pickup instructions

ABOVE LEFT You can't judge a wing chair by its upholstery! Hallmark's David Jimenez replaced the hideous Naugahyde with pristine white vinyl to fashion it into a showstopper.

ABOVE RIGHT The centerpiece of photographer Bob Greenspan's living room is a pair of Hans Wegner chairs he found in the garbage.

OPPOSITE Two ho-hum dressers get zesty when painted bright green and put together to use as a credenza.

PREVIOUS PAGES Jimenez mixed vintage with new in his 1906 Kansas City home.

to his delivery service, ending his conversation with "and leave the glass top there."

Why in the world would he buy an entire glass table and leave the useful part at the store? Ciolli pulled down his sunglasses and mumbled at me over his shoulder as we headed for the door. "Honey, those were two Maison Jansen gueridons holding up that horrible glass, and they alone are worth at least a thousand bucks apiece." And indeed they were. He used them just as he found them and created individual tables with captivating marble tops.

For most home decorators, finding an authentic Louis XIV chair or a Florence Knoll cabinet should not be a priority. Instead, set goals for finding furniture that fits into a design scheme or theme, serves a real purpose, and is structurally sound. A key to successful thrift shopping is keeping any refurbishing to a minimum. (I prefer none at all, but then I set my expectations high!) If all it takes is a coat of paint, a hearty wax job, some new hardware, or a simple refinishing, and you are willing to do it, then buy it. Whenever I see a painstaking mess of a project in the making that could cost more than it's worth, I just leave it alone. But of course, there are always exceptions, like the discovery of a piece that is obviously valuable, or one that you absolutely love and is priced right, like Ciolli's gueridons. Go ahead and buy it, and then pay a professional to restore it to your specifications.

a buyer's market

One way to evaluate a piece of furniture's worth to you is to look at comparable items sold new in other stores. A good-quality wood side chair at a middle-of-the-road, chain furniture store can run anywhere from $100 to $500, whereas a high-quality dining room table can cost at least $1,000 and a small cabinet, in the $2,000 range. When you move into the professional decorator or antiques dealer realm, those prices go up tenfold. At a thrift store, a $50 hardwood reproduction side chair in perfect condition or a 1960s dining room table for $200 that needs a good waxing is an obvious bargain. If you suspect you've found a collectable piece, do a quick Internet search for similar items, but know that any time you take opens opportunity for the next eagle-eyed shopper. My rule of thumb is that if I like it, it's useful, and it's the right price, I buy it. It just becomes a bonus when I land upon something valuable.

There are, however, some concrete ways to tell if a wood piece of furniture is durable. Avoid purchasing anything with heavily cracked or warped surfaces or that is completely destroyed or missing vital parts, such as arms or legs. Unless you know exactly how you are going to fix a broken item and plan on doing so immediately once you get it home, you are unlikely to actually make the repair. Several years ago I fell for a 1960s tufted vinyl-and-wood Swedish modern recliner that I knew had an unstable armrest. The repair is easy enough, requiring only a few drops of white glue and a wood clamp, but I've procrastinated tending to it. The result? An annoying armrest that continually swings off its peg and leaves an unsuspecting friend hanging off the edge.

Also, pay special attention to veneers, thin layers of more decorative wood applied to the surface of an inexpensive one—not necessarily a bad thing. The surface treatment has been around since ancient times and has been used in furniture making ever since. Fine antiques display intricate marquetry or wood inlays, which if done in solid wood would have been next to impossible to achieve. The issue isn't necessarily the veneer itself, but the thickness. Most furniture made before 1970 was covered in a veneer that was thick enough to endure sanding, refinishing, and touch-ups. However, most later, mass-market furniture is made with veneer so thin that it's extremely difficult to refurbish when cracked, bubbled, or torn. Even worse, some furniture makers started using veneers made of cheap paper and vinyl, again making them nearly

ABOVE RIGHT The drawers of this Belgian credenza were well made and exhibited good working hardware.

RIGHT A coat of black paint does wonders for a Thomasville buffet. When David Jimenez found it, it was in a weird cream color and had a melamine top.

LEFT A midcentury dining table and chairs sit under drive-in-movie lights that Bob Greenspan fashioned into a pair of retro hanging lamps.

ABOVE RIGHT Sometimes you can put a mirror in front of a window, especially if it's on a landing that gets light from all directions.

impossible to refinish and an assured mess if you try. When you see furniture with obviously damaged veneers, stay away unless you can live with the damage or the affected areas aren't obvious.

checking the bones

You can appraise the furniture's structure with simple tests right on the sales floor. When considering a large cabinetlike specimen, such as a dresser, an armoire, or a credenza, lean against it and give it a gentle nudging. If you can see that the frame is wobbly or loose or if it makes lots of horrible creaking noises, there's definitely a problem. Looseness of a furniture case (that's why in professional terms, they're called case goods) can cause joints to crack, eventually leading to a piece that falls apart. If you can determine how to tighten the case (maybe by firming up a screw, hammering in a nail, securing it with glue, or hiring someone outright to fix it), then it could be worth the risk of purchase. If the case good has drawers, they should slide in and out smoothly. Look for solid, hardwood drawers and avoid those with bottoms and sides made from particleboard or cheep veneers, which is usually easy to see because they don't quite match the rest of the decorative wood components. These types of drawers have a tendency to flake or fall apart. Solid-wood drawers that dovetail into their corners (where they look like they are interwoven seamlessly without the use of nails or screws) are an indication of a well-made piece of furniture.

give it a pull

Before moving on, remove as many drawers as possible so you can take a look at the guts of the piece. The drawers themselves should be in good working condition, and all internal hardware that guides them should be in place or easily repairable with a screw, nail, or glue. Corners should be held together sturdily, and bottoms should be flat and smooth. Any buckling may push the drawer's contents above its top, making it irritating to open. Remove each drawer completely from the cabinet and apply light pressure on all four sides to see if it wobbles. If there is obvious movement, then the drawer has endured much wear and tear or is of poor quality.

open wide

On furniture with doors, make sure they, too, open effortlessly and meet at the obvious angles and on level planes. If you see two doors that are clearly off-kilter, then there is a balance problem, either in the structure of the cabinet or with the hardware of the doors themselves. Doors should stay closed, either by design or by added hardware. A slightly uneven case might be the reason doors stay ajar. If door

ABOVE Intricate mitering at the corners of this wood drawer indicates a piece of furniture that is well-made.

OPPOSITE A wooden 1960s chair that when found, "was something an old aunt would buy," Jimenez says. What was once painted in off-white, flecked with gold, and covered in a funky paisley print is now a model of sophistication.

alignment isn't bothersome visually, you might consider using specially designed clips or heavy-duty magnets to solve the problem.

a fabric finish

Buy upholstered furniture with careful attention. When spying a potential purchase, there are three things to consider: the appeal of the upholstery, the comfort factor, and durability. Does it have sturdy legs and arms, clean fabric, and intact stuffing? If you can answer yes, then by all means, buy it. Let's say you've determined that the piece is structurally sound, but you just can't stand the upholstery. Cover that thing up with a custom-made slipcover in the fabric of your choice. If that's beyond your budget, premade slipcovers for almost any size and shape of chair are available at home stores and on home-shopping Web sites. A reupholstering job can cost as much as, if not more than, buying a whole new piece. One indication of upholstered furniture's quality is its weight. Try to pick it up. If it's really light, you most likely have furniture that doesn't have all the springs, extra padding, and strong structure that goes into a really good piece. Just like wood furniture, make sure the frame is sturdy. When you lean against it, or sit on it, it shouldn't wiggle or emit any creaking noises from its wood frame.

Odd sounds indicate that the frame has taken a particularly heavy beating over its lifetime, though some noise is to be expected. If you buy the piece, remember that its decorative purpose far outweighs any practical applications. Any weird sounds coming from under the fabric and ticking might point to a cracked or warped frame or broken springs, both of which are almost always beyond repair, and quite costly if not. All that internal racket may be saying, "Leave me alone!"

Persistence in finding quality pays off when shopping for thrift furniture, whether you're decorating a turn-of-the-century home, sprucing up a contemporary condo, or maintaining the integrity of a midcentury living space. A little TLC may refreshen and modernize pieces of old furniture to transform them into cherished possessions.

Falling in Love
Hallmark's David Jimenez

When David Jimenez first saw the 1906 Georgian Revival house with its pristine columns, dormer windows, and elegant portico shaded by oak trees on a double-sized lot in the Hyde Park section of Kansas City, Missouri, he knew it was the place he would call home. "It was the first house that the real estate agent showed me," says Jimenez when recalling the process that brought him from San Francisco, where he had worked for Pottery Barn and Restoration Hardware, to Kansas City in order to take the post of vice president of visual merchandising and store design for Hallmark. "When we drove by it, I told the agent to stop," he says. "And there it was, quintessentially what I imagined a home in Kansas City should look like—beautiful, stately, classic, and traditionally elegant."

His real estate dreams had come true even beyond his expectations. With its three bedrooms, living room, sitting room, library, formal dining room, dressing room, study, media room, office, and finished basement, the home is the largest place in which the New York City native has ever lived. There's a carriage house, too. "This was exactly what I wanted, but I never imagined I would find something of this scale," he says.

Jimenez's quick assessment of the house's exterior revealed that the structure had been well cared for during its lifetime: the condition of the bricks was nearly flawless, and the original copper gutters were in excellent shape and worked perfectly. Then there was the gracious portico that lured him from the street: its grand columns unblemished and its expressive moldings unchipped and intact. Once inside, Jimenez fell even harder for the house, as he marveled over woodwork that had never been painted in its hundred years and the smooth ceilings and level floors, evidence of a firm foundation resistant to years of settling. Built and originally inhabited

ABOVE LEFT In his bedroom, Jimenez placed a turn-of-the-century French armoire next to a 1960s thrift chair that he fell in love with for its Hollywood sensibility. He simply painted it black and reupholstered it in high-quality satin plumped full of goose down.

BELOW LEFT Jimenez's 1906 home in Kansas City.

by the architect Selby Kurfiss and his mother, the beloved home clearly had successive owners who continued to look after it, with its heavy, solid-wood doors and refined, crisp moldings throughout.

That's not to say the house didn't need a little updating. Jimenez carved out a luxurious spa bathroom upstairs by incorporating old closet space, and he modernized a 1980s kitchen. After these major projects and some wall painting and floor refinishing, Jimenez could then spend his time and money furnishing and decorating his new home. The cohesive visual appeal Jimenez directed is a testament to his skill of mixing the old with the new. "I love the look of antiques and thrift-store finds because they have such visual character," Jimenez says. "They make a room look collected and give it soul."

ABOVE LEFT Jimenez found a spectacular cast-iron coatrack, painted it white, and placed it on his mud porch.

ABOVE For the portico, Jimenez rewired a vintage-store lighting fixture and hung it over two thrift wing chairs that he upholstered in white vinyl.

ABOVE A marble-topped antique chest feels contemporary with current purchases from Pottery Barn, framed iconic photographs, and a vintage orb Jimenez bought at a San Francisco flea market.

OPPOSITE Jimenez's home office takes a modern turn with a Knoll Barcelona chair at a chrome-and-glass Parsons table.

Unlike many decorators who recommend starting the whole process with a fabric swatch or the colors in a rug, Jimenez, who is not a decorator but a visual merchandising professional, was guided by his desire to create rooms that elicit emotion. For inspiration, he pored over shelter magazines and home-design books, and finally decided that he would honor the existing style of his home and give it a bit of sexiness with textures and layered elements. "For instance, on the main level in the living room, I knew I wanted to give a nod to Paris in the 1960s with pretty, open chairs and an angular straight-arm sofa."

He already owned a thrift-store sofa from Palm Springs that fit that description, but then he had all these other rooms to fill. "I love watching a visual thread come together," Jimenez says. The economic advantage of living in Kansas City allowed him to stretch his decorating budget far more than if he had been embarking on the same shopping spree in San Francisco or New York. Before he started scouring thrift stores, estate sales, and antiques shops in both Palm Springs, where he has two homes, and Kansas City, he secured storage units on both coasts. "Anything I fell in love with, I bought it, photographed it, wrote a description, cataloged it, then put it in storage." Next, he created a simple organization system for his refinisher and upholsterer to follow, since there was so much furniture to tackle at one time. Furniture pieces were labeled with notes on paper to get a coat of either black or white paint. Jimenez also jotted down additional indications as to what kind of fabric would go where and which items would get the added accent of decorative nail heads. His black-and-white theme unified the rooms. The white paint highlighted furniture with interesting lines or carvings, such as a pair of 1960s Regency reproduction chairs, one of which sits in his blue guest room, and the other, as a towel stand in the upstairs bath. The black paint allows a piece to blend in a room, or to tie together similar yet different furniture designs. All the antiques kept their natural wood finish.

SOFA Jimenez re-covered what was once a hideous orange 1970s sofa and placed it into his masculine and moody Paris-inspired living room.

LIGHTING New lighting—a nickel chandelier, a crystal table lamp, and a metal, shaded piece—fits in a room that is otherwise decorated with thrift and vintage discoveries.

COFFEE TABLE A Lucite shelf once used to display a collection of toy automobiles gets tipped on its side and topped with a piece of cut glass to form a floating coffee table.

CHEST Part of a pair, a Moorish-style 1950s Dorothy Draper piece by Heritage Henredon retains its original Hollywood flair.

ARMCHAIR Once covered in eye-burning fabric, an armchair from a thrift store got a sexy French twist when Jimenez painted it black and gave it fresh upholstery.

SIDE TABLE Decorating themes need not be taken literally to evoke emotion. A thrift-store 1960s table with romantic metal legs sits well in its inviting Parisian-flavored living room.

As Jimenez embarked on his Kansas City decorating adventure, it was at an estate sale in Palm Springs that a dilapidated Chesterfield sofa first called out to him. "It was a mess," he says. "The leather was tattered and in disrepair." Nevertheless, Jimenez noted that despite the horrible look of the rest, the wood frame was in good condition. He paid $250 for the gentlemanly object and sent it off to storage to wait for its rebirth. When he needed a seating solution for his sunny mudroom off the kitchen, he thought, "Why not try the sofa in storage?" He reversed the aging process with a coat of black paint, fresh upholstery, and nail heads to complement the curls and curves of a Kansas City thrift-store find that stands across the way: a turn-of-the-century cast-iron coatrack with regal faces embedded within its winding arms. "Originally it was white and dingy with a scratched surface," he says. "I knew that I wanted something for the mudroom, and when I saw this, it looked like it could be original to the house. I also love the idea that it held umbrellas." So on went a coat of white paint and a brand-new mirror, now reflecting the reinvigorated Chesterfield sofa.

Jimenez admits to not having a meticulously laid out plan for his furniture purchases. But because he was accustomed to a fast-paced career in visual merchandising, requiring him to track multiple decorative details simultaneously and solve design dilemmas on the spot, he says he felt it all came together organically since he allowed his heart to guide him. "I just decided that if something really spoke to me, and I felt I could realistically bring it to life and the price was right, then I would buy it." When a pair of Naugahyde-covered wing chairs, one blue and the other green for $150 apiece at a Kansas City thrift store, begged his attention, he adopted them. "I loved the silhouettes, and the fact that they didn't match exactly, but complemented each other." Off came the 1970s veined Naugahyde and on went sleek white vinyl and a coat of black paint on the legs, enforcing the already established black-and-white theme. Eventually, he placed them on

the airy portico, where they reside, 365 days of the year.

Jimenez's burst of decorating was driven by a deadline he was determined to meet. During renovations, he lived in the carriage house, furnished with the midcentury pieces he brought from San Francisco. A representative of the Kansas City Alumnae chapter of the Kappa Kappa Gamma Holiday Homes Tour saw the carriage house and asked Jimenez to show off his at-the-time undecorated home during its upcoming event. Based on what she saw of his temporary décor, she didn't feel the need to see the main house complete. She made that offer in July, and Jimenez, who says he thrives under deadline, signed on. But soon the refurbishing started to drag, leaving him with only six weeks to stage and decorate four floors before the tours

ABOVE LEFT An hourglass and old industrial gears make for whimsy atop a Paul McCobb cabinet.

ABOVE The mirror placed in Jimenez's sitting room elongates the space and reflects his collection of art and photos on the adjacent wall.

began. He negotiated a deal with his contractors so that as they finished a room, he would start decorating. "Every day of the week, I would get home at five or six after a full day of work, put on the music, and have my delivery people bring over the furniture for the room I was going to decorate." He had seven sofas to place, and basically did it by trial and error, moving them from room to room until each one seemed to be in the right spot. A fine nineteenth-century Belgian armoire he spotted at a local furniture shop rotated throughout the house when Jimenez brought it home. "I fell in love with the color of the wood and the detail of the molding, but I really didn't know what I was going to do with it." Initially, he thought he'd find a space for it in the living room, but the proportions were too large. Three rooms and a floor later, he settled on his own bedroom, where he matched it with a thrift-store chair painted black and reupholstered, a French antique side table, and a mercury-glass lamp from a San Francisco thrift store. In six short weeks, Jimenez had fully decorated his home.

Now, when the jet-setter happens to be in town, he happily entertains in the home of which he is so proud. Certain affairs are known for traveling from room to room, maybe starting off in the dining area with martinis plucked from a chic black bamboo-motif server refashioned out of a yellowed, 1960s Thomasville thrift-store discovery. Then the crowd might migrate to the living room for a dishy gossip session on a glamorous yet subdued oversized sofa, which was upholstered in 1970s orange fabric when Jimenez found it at a thrift store. As the wee morning hours creep in, the gang might take a break from dancing to Latin music in the dining room and head upstairs to the sitting room, where they kick off their shoes and curl up on yet another vintage sofa. It's no surprise that guests frequently find it difficult to leave Jimenez's welcoming home, since the love and care that went into creating it is evenly spread throughout. "I had one guest say to me, 'David, I think we drank and danced in every room in your house.' And when I think of it, we did!"

Mum's the Word
Turquoise's Vanessa De Vargas

Don't even think about questioning Vanessa De Vargas about where she found that fabulous Chinese chest in her Venice Beach living room or the antique-looking side chairs in a client's bedroom. She probably won't tell you. "I can't reveal my secrets," says De Vargas, principal at LA's home design and furnishings firm Turquoise, which keeps clients coming back for more of the personalized twist she so lovingly applies to furniture.

De Vargas, a former Hollywood agent, would hate it if anyone confused her secrecy with snobbery. It's just that if she tells the competition about the garage sales, flea markets, and thrift stores she frequents, she's afraid her supply might dry up. And when working with clients who are spending good money for her expertise, it suddenly sounds less glamorous when they discover that a $15 end table—which she might have painted and equipped with new drawer pulls—has ended up in their $2-million home. Whether in a prefab, ecofriendly show house, an immunology specialist's Brentwood condo, or her own 550-square-foot Venice Beach cottage, the De Vargas touch on old furniture is known for turning what was once on sale for a few dollars on someone's lawn to a prized possession in another's home. Her hallmark of mixing vintage and thrift with new pieces from places like IKEA and West Elm makes her skills attractive to clients who look to her for design expertise that fits within their budget.

For Dr. Geemee Chung's Brentwood condo, De Vargas whipped up a concoction of eras including nineteenth-century French, Chinese

ABOVE LEFT An inoffensive wood table that Kim already had got a new personality when De Vargas added the Panton S chairs.

BELOW LEFT A Lucite box created with artist Jordan Cappella to hold De Vargas's collection of design books and serve as an end table. Next to it is a vintage Baker sofa that De Vargas covered in a tailored slipcover.

OPPOSITE Cappella made a Lucite cabinet for Jennifer Siegel's Office of Mobile Design house in Venice Beach. He used vintage Bakelite handles and old hinges to complete the piece.

ABOVE LEFT Mixing two refurbished dressers with a new mirror is a tableau that exemplifies the De Vargas touch.

ABOVE RIGHT This extra long Empire sofa took on a rocker attitude with its black vinyl upholstery and a gold-painted base at Jennifer Siegel's Office of Mobile Design house in Venice Beach. Once again, De Vargas collaborated with Cappella to create a coffee table out of an old travel trunk.

antiquity, 1960s contemporary, and today's comfort for a remedy the doctor ordered. "I wanted it to look like a New York loft," Chung says. "I didn't want lots of stuff everywhere, and I also wanted it to be comfortable because I work such long hours that when I come home, I want to relax." Chung had limited experience working with decorators, so initially she was hesitant to make drastic changes.

After painting over a wall full of garish orange and green color blocks in the living room with a neutral tone, De Vargas started to gain Chung's confidence by adding pieces little by little to her existing furniture. First came a delicate, thrift-store metal rope table, and then a Louis XVI repro-duction that De Vargas painted, recovered, and coupled with Chung's new upholstered conversational unit. The accent furniture upped the visual quotient for the room without Chung's having to endure the pains and expense of a complete overhaul. In the dining area, an innocuous, round wood table that Chung already owned got a new look when De Vargas replaced the boring, matching chairs with a set of contemporary Panton S examples that are high in both style quotient and in function. "The chairs

are great for Chung because they very easily slide under the table," De Vargas says. Sometimes, when clients are indecisive about their furniture choices, she will leave a piece of furniture with them to test-drive. On a recent visit, De Vargas was trying to convince Chung to hold on to a lovely, refurbished chair that the decorator decided was perfect for the doctor's space although she had already exceeded her decorating budget. "That's one of Vanessa's tricks. She leaves something here for a week and a half or two, and then I fall in love with it and want to keep it." But Chung stood by her guns this time and De Vargas carried the chair out to her Volvo, even though it seemed a perfect addition to the bedroom.

In De Vargas's own home, one can expect to walk in on a completely different décor at least once or twice a year. "My friends laugh at me because every time they come over, it looks different." She describes her current living space as "cozy, beachy with a touch of chinoiserie," and just as she does with her clients, she mixes old and new with unexpected colors on iconic shapes.

Her vintage Baker sofa got a light lift with a crisp, white tailored slipcover piped in black. She collaborated with Jordan Cappella, a Lucite designer, to

ABOVE The goal for De Vargas was to make Chung's apartment feel like a New York loft. She combined contemporary, new furniture with thrift finds, such as a rope table and a reproduction Louis XVI chair, which De Vargas painted and re-covered.

ABOVE Side tables in the bedroom of De Vargas's Venice Beach home brightened up with a fresh coat of white paint.

OPPOSITE De Vargas painted the Asian-themed table black and white to give it an unexpected sensation. In the corner, a Lucite box made by Cappella contains her collected design books and transforms them into a side table.

use the clear material to box in De Vargas's collection of decorating books that span the decades. "I went a little eBay happy and bought a ton. I don't look at them all the time, but I still wanted to display them, so the Lucite side tables became a great storage idea." In keeping with the Asian theme, she took an old, low-to-the-ground coffee table with subtly curved angles that she found for a few dollars at a thrift store and painted it three-quarters black and the rest white. "I guess it would be very predictable to see the table lacquered in one color, so I chose two," De Vargas says. "It's a little unexpected."

For Jennifer Siegel's Office of Mobile Design prefab show house nearby, De Vargas teamed up again with Cappella to create an interior completely at odds with what one might imagine in the sparse, contemporary setting. De Vargas and Cappella again looked to Lucite, this time to form a functional table that shows off a vintage piece of luggage. But the pièce de résistance is a 12-foot-long Empire sofa reproduction, a thrift-store purchase that now commands the entire end of one bright, sunny room. For De Vargas, this find was rare, since often pieces of this proportion are in poor condition due to the added stress and strain on their wooden frames. Its dimensions attract such attention that upholstery had to be chosen either to accentuate or diminish its presence. A solid fabric would help it blend in, whereas a pattern might make it stand out too much. "We were looking for a punk rock look," De Vargas says. They sprayed gold paint on its wood base and covered it in large sheaths of shiny, black vinyl, giving the settee just the right amount of attitude in a sparsely decorated room. Whether punk rock or China chic, every De Vargas design project becomes a glowing example of her affection for incorporating high-quality used furniture. "Since my inspiration as a designer comes largely from the past, there is so much emotion in furniture that has seen so much." Through De Vargas, forgotten, cast-off furniture, when treated to a coat of lime green paint or dressed up with Lucite drawer pulls, gains a whole new identity for the future.

California Dreaming
Interiors Photographer Bob Greenspan

Photographer Bob Greenspan's home looks as if it could have been funneled right out of Southern California, lovingly lifted cross-country, and laid down on a subdivided plot of land in Overland Park, Kansas. That is unless it's covered in a blanket of snow and dripping in icicles more commonly associated with the harsh winters that blast their way through the Midwest. But on a sparkly, sun-streaked day, the light beams through the floor-to-ceiling windows of Greenspan's 1957 home, designed by the LA architectural firm A. Quincy Jones and Frederick Emmons. Donald Drummond, a native Californian who moved to Kansas City after World War II and is widely credited with bringing modern-designed homes to the area, built Greenspan's house.

The house, with its many large panes of glass and angular, contemporary lines, caught this lensman's eye, despite the utter state of neglect in which he found it. Thirty-year-old green shag carpeting covered much of the floors, the kitchen had its original cabinets, and the appliances dated back to the 1970s. There was no drywall in the house, and every wall was covered with paneling just nailed to the studs. Then there was the dismal state of the yard. "I probably removed more than fifty trees that had grown wild from seedlings that grew like weeds," he says. "It wasn't until the second year here that I finally made it out to the far corner of the backyard, and discovered a grove of bamboo growing there."

ABOVE LEFT A look into Greenspan's A. Quincy Jones–designed home.

BELOW LEFT Sputnik-era clocks, a neon letter, and a collection of Edison bulbs accent Greenspan's fiery red fireplace.

OPPOSITE, ABOVE The angular architecture of Greenspan's midcentury home stands out in a Midwest development of 1960s colonial and ranch houses.

OPPOSITE, BELOW One of Greenspan's treasured globes.

His creative vision, and a lot of elbow grease, is finally paying off; the house now has a clean, open feeling that the architects sought to convey in their original designs. "The house almost has a Jetsons meets Brady Bunch feel," he says. "I've always had a thing for contemporary and midcentury design, and it seemed just right." Greenspan and his wife, Amy, have stayed true to their home's soul when selecting both old and new furniture, always giving a wink and a nod to the past, with items found at their favorite antiques malls, thrift and vintage stores, and even from the garbage, often resulting in finds that would make collectors envious.

When a local bank was going through a gut job, Greenspan noticed a Dumpster full of discarded junk. But then was it? As he rummaged through the detritus, he came upon a pair of chairs with subtly turned lines that reminded him of Danish pieces from the 1960s. Without hesitation, he

tossed them into the back of his car and carted them home. After a little research on the Internet and talking with local experts, he discovered that what he dug out of the trash was a Hans Wegner design, simply known as The Chair. It is the same style of furniture that was used during the 1960 debates between John F. Kennedy and Richard Nixon. The two refinished side chairs now sit in the Greenspans' living room.

Greenspan was stumped to find a bathroom vanity that fit his house's modern mood and was convinced he could find an appropriate dresser and drop a sink into it. "It took a little looking, but I eventually found a piece that looked like it could have come straight out of a 1950s bedroom," he says. "I think I paid about $285 for it at Boomerang [a local vintage store]." For pure decoration, Greenspan selected futuristic, atomic clocks from the '50s and '60s and an illuminated neon sign bought for the love of his life, Amy. He found the gigantic *A* at an antiques mall in Harrisville, Missouri.

Other collections include a grouping of globes sitting atop a sliding-door wardrobe. In the kitchen bar area, there's a corner filled with tiki mugs, a pursuit that his wife instigated. "They remind us of fun, swankier times, although neither of us was around during the heyday. They also make me think of warm, exotic places, and enjoying a drink by the beach as the sun sets and Martin Denny music is playing in the background."

To further play up the 1950s sensibility, Greenspan salvaged several red-and-white candy-striped lighting fixtures that once illuminated the entry of an old drive-in movie theater, and he hung them upside down over a midcentury R-Way table and matching chairs in the dining room. He found the set at a local vintage shop, Retro Inferno, where he paid a few hundred dollars for them, a price much lower than a new reproduction that would run at least $1,000.

The Heartland home has undergone a complete makeover; a frigid breeze no longer leaks through the once-uninsulated walls, and furniture that might have at one time been undesirable is a focal point of authenticity and imagination. A wireless Apple TV system now supplies the exotic sounds of Les Baxter, but the old neon signs are just as vibrant as they were decades ago.

TOP The exterior of Bob Greenspan's A. Quincy Jones home in Overland Park, Kansas.

ABOVE When Greenspan couldn't find a bathroom vanity to suit him, he bought a 1950s piece of furniture and had a sink fitted into it

OPPOSITE Greenspan lights up his vintage dining table with collected pieces of neon signs and a pair of red-and-white-striped lamps that used to illuminate a drive-in theater.

THE TRANSFORMERS: Decorator Mark Ciolli of Carl & Co. Gives a Belgian Credenza an Haute Couture Face-Lift, and *This Old House*'s Alex Bandon Applies a Touch of Chic to a Set of Thrift-Store Chairs

CIOLLI'S HIGH-END CHALLENGE

When one of Mark Ciolli's wealthy clients spotted a bright red, lacquered $86,000 Andre Arbus credenza that she absolutely adored but that, even for her, was way beyond what she wanted to spend, it was up to Ciolli to re-create a functional piece of furniture at a fraction of the cost.

He started out by purchasing an 82-inch-long 1930s Belgian credenza, which was a good piece to start with: it was fully constructed with dovetailed and mitered joints, and the drawer knobs and sabots were made of bronze and appeared to be in good condition. Once the credenza arrived at Osmundo Echevarria's Manhattan studio (recently relocated to Queens), the hardware was removed and the piece was prepared for a good sanding. The doors were taken off, and each was enhanced with a plaque signifying one of the four seasons. And then came some more sanding and the lacquer. Finally the studio goldwashed the bronze hardware, added golden details, and lined the shelves and drawers with Venetian paper, creating a regal piece of furniture fit for a royal.

ABOVE LEFT The Osmundo Echevarria studio goldwashed the bronze hardware and lined the drawers and shelves in fine Venetian paper.

OPPOSITE, ABOVE It didn't bother Ciolli that the marble top of his vintage Belgian credenza broke in delivery. He was going to toss it anyway, since his vision for the piece was more Asian chic than country French.

OPPOSITE, BELOW The completed credenza with coats of red lacquer gives a design nod to one made by André Arbus.

TOP A set of 1960s wood chairs awaits their transformation into a prized furniture possession.

ABOVE After applying a coat of primer, Bandon carefully applied a coat of bright red paint.

OPPOSITE Bandon's finished product is ready for its debut in her neighbor's new apartment.

BANDON'S MISSION

When Alex Bandon, *This Old House* editor, heard that her neighbor, Pamela Cederquist, wanted to inject some color into her new 500-square-foot, one-bedroom apartment, she stepped up to the challenge. Bandon spotted a set of six 1960s wicker-and-wood chairs at Housing Works for $129, which was a real steal. "It hit me that red lacquer would both give Pamela the pop of color that she wanted and imbue the chairs with a modernized Asian feel," says Bandon. Then she went for a bold geometric print fabric for the seat to beef up the modern aspect. "And voilà," says Bandon, "Grandma chic!"

ALEX BANDON'S TEN TIPS TO A NEW CHAIR

1. Remove the seats by unscrewing them from underneath.
2. Lightly sand the chairs with a 150-grit sandpaper to provide a surface that will hold the paint.
3. Prime the chairs with an oil-based primer. (On untreated surfaces, use a primer only when necessary. If you're unsure, paint a test area. Let it dry completely and then press on a strip of masking tape and let it sit for ten minutes. If the paint comes off when you briskly rip off the tape, then you need a primer. Never prime wicker, as it easily gums up.)
4. Once the primer dries, sand the chairs again to further ensure a smooth painting surface.
5. Paint one coat of oil-based, high-gloss paint, making sure not to use too much paint at once. Oil-based paints make for hard finishes, but use high-gloss latex if necessary.
6. Sand again with 220-grit sandpaper, and paint a second coat, being careful to avoid drips and paint strokes.
7. Paint the wicker backs in high-gloss black paint with an artist's brush.
8. Meanwhile, remove old fabric from seats, and add foam if they need more cushioning.
9. Attach the fabric to the seats with a staple gun, using ¼-inch staples. Start from the center of one side with a staple, then pull the fabric taut on the opposite side and staple there. Work out from the center to keep the fabric tight.
10. Once the pieces are dry, screw the seats back on, and put the new chairs to use.

accessories

in the details

Think of the details in a room in the same way you prepare
to get dressed every day. You start with a canvas made of all
the basics: a suit and shirt, a dress, or even a pair of jeans and
a sweater. That navy suit and crisp, white dress shirt burst to
life when you add a rich necktie, some silver cuff links, and
a pocket square. A slinky evening dress becomes red-carpet
material when it's matched with a pair of dangling earrings, a
glittery necklace, and sexy heels. Even a pair of good-old blue
jeans looks naked without an appropriate belt that adds just that
special spark of interest. Accessories pull together your furniture
elements with a unifying thread of color, texture, or theme.

ABOVE Every piece of porcelain in Randall Beale's collection comes with a story. The parakeets (top right) remind him of his Gramma Lil, who had a similar pair sitting on her piano.

OPPOSITE The appeal of set designer Peter Frank's home is partly due to his ability to arrange incongruous items for a consistent look. Atop a collectable Edward Wormley chest from Drexel Heritage, vintage and thrift items that relate in shape and color are grouped harmoniously.

PREVIOUS PAGES A trio of flea-market Marcello Fantoni canisters enlivens a countertop in Alison Attenborough and Jamie Kimm's stylish kitchen.

Curated collections, wall décor, mirrors, and soft home accessories found in thrift stores express personality in a room where guests become acquainted with the person who lives there.

Thrift discoveries can spark a collection that evokes memory, stimulates imagination, and offers the feeling of a curated home. If you have a collection, celebrate it, says *Apartment Therapy*'s Maxwell Gillingham-Ryan. "Put them on a pedestal," he says. "Make certain to highlight them in a room so they become part of a decorative element." Some people refer to a collection as a vignette—a group of items that when put together offer a snapshot of a personal history or a dedicated theme. Cull collections from almost any concept—from a specific color and texture of glass that forms an attractive unit to a group of baseball caps, which Gillingham-Ryan recalls pulling from the overpacked closet of one client to display in an area where he could actually see and enjoy them. When grouped together, collections pack a design wallop, but when its parts are strewn about carelessly, they can often look junky.

When thrift shopping for home accessories, creating a collection can help focus your hunt. Because of the massive amounts of merchandise to choose from, it's easy to be distracted by an item (especially when it's gorgeous, precious, and a bargain) that doesn't quite fit into an established idea and is destined to throw you off a consistent track. Say, for instance, I decided to plop a single wood Arts and Crafts candlestick into my mix of colorful glass and bright porcelain. It might work, if the color tones are the same, but off the top of my head, I can't see how any addition lacking a luminescent quality, let alone the brightness factor, would accent my already established collection, so I would either buy it for a separate grouping or leave it in the store.

Randall Beale, half of the Beale-Lana design team, grouped oversized, faceted stones that gleam and glisten among his mostly black-and-white-themed apartment. "There is nothing more beautiful than the light reflection of faceted stone," Beale says. "I've always been attracted to the reflection of light and shine." The effect is glamorous and captivating, even though the stones are of different shapes and sizes. To further dramatize Beale's ambitions, the light-catching pieces fuel additional star

power when positioned upon an antique silver tray. He continues his glitz fest across the room with a '70s disco ball that rests on a backdrop of a black-and-white Piero Fornasetti screen. Again, he was consistent in his collecting mission, both in texture and tone, to serve up visual interest that shines from any vantage point in the room. The shiny pieces add whimsy to a boxy, 1960s apartment building and add a light touch to the fine art and photography displayed throughout.

reflecting the past

Allow the premise of creating visual groupings to spread right up to your walls. Thrift-store mirrors already have an innate reflective quality that makes them perfect candidates for showing off together as a unit. You can further enhance the cohesiveness of multiple mirrors by painting all the frames in a single color, lessening attention to the individual moldings and shapes, and increasing attention to the overall creation. A coat of paint diverts attention from imperfections, such as scrapes or chips common among thrift-store frames. When deciding on where to place mirrors, either in collected groups or singly, consider what will appear in their reflections, as properly positioned mirrors can glorify areas of interest in a room and help visually expand the space. However, a messy library, a pile of newspapers, or a jumble of knickknacks highlighted in the looking glass can make a room feel unplanned and claustrophobic.

Wall art, either framed or painted on a canvas, is so plentiful in thrift stores that it can often be had for only a few dollars. At the same time, be prepared to dig around until you find the right merchandise for your home. Thrift stores rarely have enough space to hang them for easy viewing, so they are usually stacked or piled out of the way, making them difficult to see at first glance. Again, when buying wall décor, your decorating experience will be more satisfying once you establish a theme, which could be a subject matter, a color, or a medium. A broad theme, such as flowers, boats, or even cathedrals, can help you narrow your hunt as you collect varied shapes and sizes of these subjects and group them together as a visual unit. Use the same criteria when considering abstract acrylics, string art, fashion sketches, paint-by-numbers, or even cross-stitched or hand-embroidered designs. As always, keep your color story at hand when choosing wall décor. Lean toward examples that coordinate, either by creating a stark contrast or a mellow blending, with the hues you've selected for your walls. And finally, make sure that any prospective wall-décor purchase accents the existing furniture and floor coverings you've established as the basics for the room. Once you get home and start combining your collected finds, a dramatic design element will start to appear—one that delights the eye and invites intrigue.

objects of desire

Sometimes an object, as long as it complements your basics, can stand alone. A large turn-of-the-century mirror, by itself, can enliven a clean wall scape. A single piece of thrift pottery placed on a stark, modern table can enhance the sleekness of its surroundings. A gigantic abstract painting over a sofa or a table may be the only element you need on the wall. Window treatments, such as draperies or shades, highlighting a stupendous view may be so jaw-dropping that anything else could be just too much. Play with the idea of scale, and experiment with the unlikely. Put a gigantic candlestick in the middle of a series of minuscule ones, or within a set of round ceramics, drop in one bold square example to attract attention. Think of placing accessories as if you are creating an urban skyline. The dips between the buildings add interest among the skyscrapers, but the overall effect is awe inspiring.

ABOVE Sometimes items like this already curated set of pink flamingos from the Handel/Wendt garage sale can't help but say, "Take me home!"

lighten up

Adding portable lighting to a room develops a dimension that can focus attention on a special area of the home or, at the same time, pull the eye away from the less desirable. When you think of lighting, remember, it can also be purely decorative, like an exotic Venetian chandelier, or functional, like a metal reading lamp. Decide what you're going to use it for first, since poring over your favorite novel under the glow of that

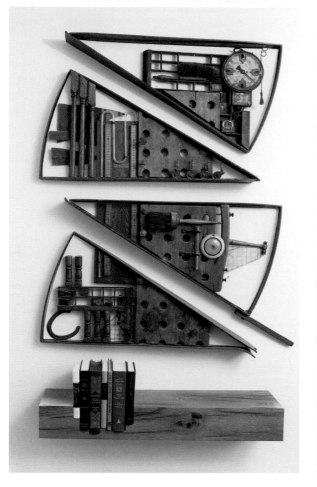

ABOVE LEFT Designer John Bartlett and framer John Esty gathered tools, pieces of wood, and an old clock and framed them in angular terrazzo molds.

ABOVE RIGHT A set of supersized cocktail glasses at Housing Works are sure to make your next party a boozy affair, according to Simon Doonan of Barneys New York.

OPPOSITE Designer John Derian papered his foyer with pages from a vintage book that had fallen apart.

romantic chandelier may sound utterly chic, but your vision will suffer. You'll be happier with a plain old reading lamp. Like wall décor, lighting is so plentiful in thrift stores that you should plan on making multiple visits before finding a style that's right for you. As you move your eye beyond a yellowed and torn shade or broken wires that tumble out of the base, you'll start to focus on the beauty, the color, and the texture of a lamp's body. Look for base colors and metal finishes that complement existing furnishings, and seek shapes that fit in with your theme. A globular resin lamp from the 1950s might be a lot of fun, but it won't fit into every décor.

As you learn to appreciate thrift-store lighting, avoid bases that are obviously cracked and damaged, but don't instantly turn away from one whose components might seem wobbly. Since many lamps are made of multiple components that are screwed together, see if tightening them on

OPPOSITE Satisfying her passion for items that can be counted and objects from France, Heather Chadduck placed vintage liquor decanters atop French accounting ledgers.

the spot can increase stability. Ruined sockets and frayed electrical cords can easily be replaced, provided you have the know-how or are willing to hand the simple task over to an electrician. Shade selection is a personal preference, but general guidelines promote selecting one that is two-thirds the size of the base and that extends about a half inch beyond it. This usually provides an attractive proportion that hides all the fixtures underneath. Typically, round shades go with round bases and square shades with square bases. There are exceptions, such as when mixing a circular shade with a square, space-age midcentury specimen, but stick to these dimensions and you'll never fail.

this side of soft

Soft home accessories found in a thrift store add plushness, comfort, and texture to your home. They take the edge off of any hard surfaces or angles and complement upholstered furniture with their softness. Taking the collected route is a good way to amass a pillow arrangement that looks specifically tailored to your design dreams. Tie your group together with color or motif, making sure the additions accent your furniture, and mix and match sizes and shapes to create an appealing, unified design. Make your own pillows and cushions out of large pieces of fabric that can be refashioned from other home textiles; cast-off draperies, bedspreads, quilts, napkins, and tablecloths can be transformed into thought-provoking pillows or seat cushions. While in a thrift store, always flip through the apparel racks for clothes that can become fabulous home accessories. I love rummaging through snaking masses of old ties at thrift stores, always imagining uses beyond tying one of the slivers of fabric around my neck. Novel curtain tiebacks? Piping for place mats? A sophisticated patchwork pillow? A soft, knotted napkin ring?

Thrift-store accessories, whether printed 1960s tablecloths; framed, turn-of-the-century botanical prints; or stately pewter candleholders and pitchers, will add instant charm to a new atmosphere, or accentuate the old and pay homage to the past.

A World of Its Own
Designer John Derian

John Derian is a master of mining beauty in the threadbare and brandishing his golden touch to elevate the craft of decoupage to an art form and a successful design business. "People always ask me, 'What did you do when you were a kid?'" Derian says, standing on the creaky, uneven floors in the living room of his 550-square-foot New York apartment. The answer? Rearrange furniture in his 1800s childhood home in Cambridge, Massachusetts; make crafts with whatever attracted him; stencil glass; paint; build forts; and draw. The Lower East Side tenement he has called home since 1992 is a testament to his innate sense of glorifying the *trouvé,* celebrating the chipped and tarnished, and allowing the past to glide in to cast its time-honored patina on every furnishing he brings into his life.

When embarking on a thrift journey largely relegated to finer flea markets, antiques shops, and estate sales, Derian never starts out with a laundry list of what he's shopping for. "I may have a mental image of what I may 'need,' but I never go looking for it. I let things come to me." So when he's at a flea market or estate sale, he wastes no time wondering how he's going to refurbish one of his discoveries. Instead, he prefers to preserve the sentiment of the state in which he found them. With open arms, he accepts mirrors with splotchy mercury; spindly, decades-worn lusters lacking crystal drops; and metal French tables scarred with nicks and bruises, exactly as they are. For Derian, to alter them overtly would only denude them of the historic splendor that attracted him in the first place. Instead, he boasts of his relics, dents, dings and all, on the pedestal of a home he hasn't painted in more than a decade. The warm yellow walls are now bubbled and cracked, spotted with white spackling—war wounds

ABOVE LEFT This early-1800s cabinet hanging on a weathered kitchen wall holds some of Derian's vintage dishes.

BELOW LEFT The turn-of-the-century sofa from a French flea market is placed to the right of an industrial tub Derian turned over to use as a side table. Artist Peter Gee's paint palette becomes a colorful addition to Derian's wall décor.

from the recently updated electrical system. The ceiling in the dining room is marred by a circular brown mark where water once leaked in, and chunks of plaster have completely fallen out of a corner in the kitchen wall. To give the place a face-lift would strip it of its charm, so he accentuates these age spots with rusty sparkle, sun-faded color, and ageless wit. "There's life in everything," he says. "Having items around is a positive thing. They speak to you." And Derian listens.

His living room is a combination of fine antiques lightened with an unexpected flourish gleaned from flea markets. A nineteenth-century blotched French mirror puffs its status near a turn-of-the-century marble bowl of fruit. Vintage feed sacks become pillows; a crusty industrial tub acquired from the Brimfield, Massachusetts,

ABOVE LEFT Derian's beloved collected objects are displayed in a *trouvé* fashion.

ABOVE RIGHT A Chinese lantern missing its paper shade hangs next to an 1800s luster that Derian wired for a lightbulb.

ABOVE Vintage kitten cutouts are framed above a sturdy table that was originally created as an industrial mold.

OPPOSITE Seashells, pottery, silver vases, pewter cups, and china pieces all come together harmoniously under Derian's watch. A 1930s wind chime dangles from the knob of the antique china cabinet.

flea market, when tipped upside down, serves as a side table; an old corded boat fender functions quite well as a textured footstool. The accents in the room, from the framed paintings and art displayed askew on the opposite wall to the assorted pillows on the sofas, play up the fact that while major antique pieces abound, he doesn't take it all too seriously. The balance between the precious and the fanciful is pitched perfectly throughout his alluring space.

The whimsy wanders on into the dining room, where a Chinese lantern stripped of its paper hangs in the same space as a mid-1800s luster that begged for Derian to drop a lightbulb in it. When he found it impossible to achieve the pretty, creamy shade that he imagined for the adjacent foyer, he literally hit the books for a design solution. The revised option came out of a pile of broken-down nineteenth-century books and magazines about flowers that he uncovered at a flea market in Salem, Massachusetts. With little more than a bottle of Elmer's glue and water, he took the loose pages and applied them to the walls and front door to create the kind of covering that doesn't come in a roll.

Most of the details Derian added to his home were from one era or another, common household objects that have had the good fortune to end up in his possession: the 1930s hand-painted wind chime hanging from a knob on his 1850s glass-and-wood cabinet; a wooden doormat that he uses as a display board for his favorite photographs, notes, and drawings; an 1800s stoneware pitcher that now holds a fragrant spring bouquet. For in Derian's inspiring dreamscape, forgotten items reappear in the present and those that are far from pristine achieve perfection.

Subtlety Aside
Interior Designers Randall Beale and Carl Lana

Randall Beale and Carl Lana pride themselves on making unforgettable interior statements with details. So when venturing into the Upper East Side apartment of the Beale half of the Beale-Lana design team, prepare for an in-your-face barrage of big-name photographs, eighteenth-century marble sculptures, one-of-a kind contemporary art structures, creatures made of porcelain, disco and soccer balls, and Japanese plush toys. "There is nothing subtle about me," Beale says. "There never has been, and there never will be." While the variety of textures and shapes he collects in his home might appear incongruous without Beale's skilled touch, he's unified them with consistent color themes throughout, adding visual interest with splashes of the unexpected, either in scale, color, or humor.

The duo describes their work aesthetic as bad-boy chic, accented with high contrast, quality, and comfort. Staying true to his E3 ("exquisite, edgy, and elegant") philosophy, Beale has assembled a visual kaleidoscope that gently guides the eye from detail to detail. His tenacious attention to unusual objects with tactile qualities allows him to secure tempting treasures from all over the globe, both old and new, thrift and antique.

A standout example in Beale's home is a dramatic black-and-white corner in his living room, cast upon a $65 wood thrift table he painted white. At the back of the table, he placed a black Ching dynasty lamp that he salvaged from a Florida junk shop and freshened up with a white linen shade trimmed in black. Its dominant position among other black vases and vessels intensifies an appealing, unified shape that becomes the background for a white candleholder shaped like a tree branch by Ted Muehling for Nymphenburg and a white, fragile, one-of-a kind Sèvres rose he carried home from Paris. The result is a cohesive-looking group of objects that have little in common other than the two colors. "Like my life, my personal spaces just evolve," Beale says. "I enjoy trying new things, and the contradictions emerge." Throughout his home, Beale mixes collectable and priceless pieces with items that others might deem just trinkets, resulting in a happy space that's full of stories and memories.

LEFT A nondescript Housing Works table that Beale bought for $65 ("We will not discuss what it cost to refinish," he says), gets royal treatment on the top with a Ching dynasty lamp from a junk shop in Florida, a Sèvres rose from Paris, and a Baccarat poodle that was a gift from Carl Lana.

OPPOSITE A Roman bust of Caesar Augustus stands watch over Randall Beale's collection of photographs, which includes work by Cecil Beaton, Billy Name, and Ron Galella. For a pop of color and whimsy, Beale added a Cameroon Juju headdress.

His and Hers
Jonamor Décor's Senor and Jonona Amor

When an LA deejay who grew up down the street from Michael Jackson in Encino, California, and a performance artist/actress from Lubbock, Texas, fall head over heels for each other and move into a 900-square-foot duplex within shouting distance of Los Angeles High School, the creative combination is bound to burst into a home décor fusion like no other.

Senor Amor, who comes from a jet-set family accustomed to having its house "professionally decorated," he says, and Jonona Amor, who after seeing a performance of *The Nutcracker* at the age of seven developed an obsession with sleeping in a bedroom with red velvet curtains and a matching canopy, are a love match made in thrift-store heaven. Their LA home, which Jonona describes as Aztec modern, is a temple to cacophonous assortments of taxidermy animals, bright orange accents, dismembered dolls, a gigantic futuristic painting, turn-of-the century infant photographs, leather feline heads, and a sleek pastiche of 1960s and 1970s furniture. While it may sound like a mishmashed mouthful of motifs crammed under one roof, that description couldn't be farther from the truth. Her graceful touch weaves a color theme throughout and breaks up the visual stimuli with more sober furniture to effect a style that is absolutely harmonious.

Senor Amor, who operates Retropia, a Hollywood art gallery and home design shop with Jonona and A. Lori Tucci, attributes his affection for buying used goods to having spent the past twenty years scouring thrift stores for records to add to his collection. Retropia recently launched Jonamor Décor, a decorating firm dedicated to formulating home designs that show off the couple's quest to live in surroundings that revere the charm and wit of the 1960s and 1970s. As long as a thrift- or flea-market find is of good condition and an interesting shape, then it's prime picking for either their own home or for one of their design clients. "That's great if a piece of furniture happens to have a label or a designer name and is a good deal," Senor Amor says. "But it doesn't have to be that. We get a lot more satisfaction from finding, say, a great chrome rocking chair for $60. Done!"

ABOVE LEFT In the kitchen, Jonona Amor found vintage fabric for the curtains that coordinates with the thrift-store lighting fixture. On the windowsill, a coffee canister missing its lid turns into a planter and a sassy lady planter becomes an art brush holder.

ABOVE RIGHT A desk, already decoupaged in a map of the world, made its way into the Amors' home office.

Their home is packed with some of the best examples of flea-market and thrift finds from all over the West Coast. When they set their sights on an item they've just got to have—say, a complete light wood bedroom suite located in a Palm Springs thrift store—there's no stopping them. They just rent a U-Haul and bring it on home along with the rest of their stash to either add to their own collections or save for a client. A visitor to the couple's home has to stop and take a long, deep breath before delving into the method of their melodious madness, but soon realizes that the way they parlay their message is by grouping their favorite accessories into digestible vignettes that speak to their eccentric interests.

Senor Amor, who has used this Mexicanized name since high school, is intrigued by memorabilia paying tribute to Shriners Masonic societies. "I think it all started with the Grand Poobah on the *Flintstones*," he says. "And then when I started going to thrift stores, there was all this Shriners memorabilia that fascinated me. I loved the idea that it was a secret brotherhood of old guys, and the symbolism spoke to me." On a shelf in the entryway, he congregated tasseled, felt Fez caps with statuettes commemorating his beloved Masons for a masculine display sure to evoke a grin. On the opposing shelf, Jonona went girly-girl with a smorgasbord of fake food—ice cream sundaes, deviled eggs, a pastrami sandwich, and a mini chocolate doughnut—once used in restaurant displays. "I had collected so many old cookbooks from the fifties and sixties that I couldn't buy any more," she says. "So I started buying the fake food that reminded me of those beautiful old pictures in those cookbooks. And then when I really started to try to eat more healthy foods, these represented the things that I would no longer allow myself to have."

The fireplace mantel in the living room is covered with a menagerie of décor that, when viewed individually, appears entirely incongruous: taxidermy animals, blowfish, wood and metal figurines, and a pair of Victorian-style, 1970s candlesticks. However, Jonona Amor balanced symmetry, color, and shape to create an engaging presentation, which is evident throughout their home.

"I was always into decorating my room," she says of her standout penchant for incorporating the odd, the beautiful, and quite often the morbid. After her mother surprised the seven-year-old with the rich, red antebellum bedroom of her dreams, Jonona innocently decorated her plush surroundings with finds from a family trip to Mexico. "I bought all these tacky, feathered roach clips and decorated the canopy of my bed with them," she says. "Can you imagine?" For every out-there object that she finds intriguing, she still finds herself drawn to romantic and Victorian-inspired thrift-store finds, such as the ceramic bust of a pretty woman wearing pearls that holds her paintbrushes above the kitchen sink and the pink wicker chair where she work on her designs. She credits many of her design influences to old movies. "One time, she watched *Gone With the Wind* every day for an entire month," says Señor Amor.

ABOVE Jonona Amor opted for vintage posters and prints with the same color themes and unified them with simple black frames and white mats to hang in the couple's ladylike bathroom.

ABOVE Jonona's contribution to the his-and-hers collection: fake foods that she's collected over the years.

OPPOSITE A thread of the color orange weaves its way through the Amors' home. On the mantel, Jonona symmetrically placed dissimilar objects, taxidermy animals, and curvy glass-and-metal sculptures, all from thrift stores and flea markets, above a 1970s bamboo bar cart.

Likewise, his taste has never conformed to the expected, either. During the '70s, he recalls incorporating the rainbow from the now-defunct teen magazine *Dynamite* into his childhood bedroom, in a household where the den had an African theme with leather sofas and the living room felt fresh out of the French countryside. His parents' chamber was a modern work of chrome and Lucite. In the early '80s at the age of sixteen, Senor Amor moved with his family to Paris and set about creating another stylish bedroom scenario, which featured black carpeting, black walls, a white vinyl egg chair, and a bubble lamp. "I was modern and I didn't even know it." Senor Amor admits that it took Jonona's feminine touch to civilize his single-living days, especially when it came to a 9 x 5-foot futuristic painting that now hangs above the 1960s metal-and-glass dining table the couple hauled home from Palm Springs. The dark and mysterious painting leaned for years against the wall of his former bachelor pad. "I mean, I thought it was cool, but Jonona pushed me to hang it up when she moved in." Together, the Amors have created a home out of seemingly dissimilar elements and turned their design passion into a business where their distinct personalities complement each other.

"I deal with all the residents and logistical issues, whereas she's the creative talent," Senor Amor says. "I'm the people person who makes things go from points A and B to C, but Jonona's the one who draws beautifully and creates these incredible concepts out of her imagination."

A Feast for the Eyes
Food Stylist Alison Attenborough and Chef Jamie Kimm

Alison Attenborough and Jamie Kimm have found the key to negotiating a personal style in their 1,800-square-foot Manhattan loft even when their design tastes, at first mention, might seem to be completely opposed. He likes sleek and clean. She tends toward bright colors and bold prints.

In some marriages, such differences might signal disaster. But in the case of Attenborough, one of the nation's top food stylists, and Kimm, a food consultant and personal chef, the result is similar to a tasty dish where the sweet complements the savory. "The only color I don't like is no color," Attenborough says. "I love pinks, purples, and aqua." On the

contrary, Kimm tends to lean toward simple lines and subtler tones. When Attenborough propped out the couple's shiny, stainless-steel kitchen with cooking utensils and canisters, Kimm walked in demanding to know why these things were left on the counter. The compromise? The furniture is modern, with creations by Harvey Probber and Eames, while the accessories are bright and bold, accented by sunny, bright geometrics and swirls associated with Pucci and Missoni prints.

There's plenty of color and transparent glass textures to give an edge to the quieter wood furniture. In the bedroom a white Eames chair is accented with thrift pillows and brightly hued art and photographs. Visitors who look closely will note the couple's wedding picture, shot by Annie Leibowitz, on display near a catchy, graphic Gary

RIGHT Attenborough at work in the New York loft that she shares with her husband. She made pillows out of a vintage Pucci printed cape and and put them on her Harvey Probber sofa, also a thrift find.

OPPOSITE, LEFT Colorful glass and a floral arrangement sit atop a flea-market table.

OPPOSITE, RIGHT Attenborough's love of color shows in her collection of bright glass. Matchbooks with appealing designs add interest to this glass parfait dish.

FOLLOWING PAGES, LEFT A tall flea-market stool strikes an appealing contrast against the sleek and modern stainless-steel kitchen. **RIGHT** Color arrives to the counter with a curvy blue canister, a playful Marcello Fantoni dachshund, and an Austrian coffee tin.

ABOVE Transparent colored glass, all flea-market or thrift finds, add a dreamy, luminescent quality to a modern setting.

OPPOSITE Patience pays off. Attenborough proves that shopping with an open mind and good vision has its benefits. An Eames chair gets a zap of color with matching pillows that Attenborough found on two separate thrift-shopping occasions.

Hume piece. Other than the boldface names whose work appears on the walls and the top-of-the-line stainless-steel appliances in the kitchen, practically everything in the Attenborough/Kimm household is the result of a thrift-store or flea-market stop. Her passion for finding previously owned goods has become one of her favorite pastimes. "When we went away to Puglia, one of the first things I wanted to know was if there were any flea markets around," Attenborough says.

Attenborough doesn't limit her shopping to decorative home details and furniture; she also maintains quite a wardrobe filled with vintage clothing as well. When she found a large, Pucci printed cape, she immediately snapped it up. "I just loved it," she says. People who know Attenborough say that of anyone, she's the kind of confident personality who is able to sport such an arresting piece of attire. Along with a set of Arne Jacobsen cutlery, again from a flea-marketing adventure, the Pucci cape rates high among her finds. Its bursts of bright hues and curlicued shapes printed on fine silk were a natural for Attenborough's own wardrobe, but you won't find her wearing that treasure anymore. It has since been turned into a set of accent pillows that add zest to the couple's contemporary sitting area. In the Attenborough/Kimm household, it's all about taking someone else's castoffs and turning them into a delicious prized possession.

Getting Crafty in the Village
Designer John Bartlett and Framer John Esty

When a beloved menswear designer moved in with one of the best picture framers in Manhattan, their home was bound to become a hotbed of creativity, anytime, day or night.

John Bartlett, the designer, and John Esty, the framer, took handmade decorating to a whole new level in their 1,000-square-foot, two-bedroom apartment in the heart of Greenwich Village. "John was relentless in getting the place together," Bartlett says of Esty. "I would wake up at seven a.m. to the sound of his making cabinets and drilling holes."

But before Bartlett and Esty made the gigantic leap to move in together, they sat down and combed through each and every one of their possessions, deciding which ones would make their way into the new space, and which ones would be passed on to Housing Works. "Our tastes are very much in sync," Bartlett says. "We both love big furniture, found objects, and lots of art." Moving into a new environment also gave Bartlett and Esty the opportunity to evaluate which of their individual possessions might need repurposing or refreshening to fit into the new space. "John is a master framer, so everything that I had was reframed," Bartlett says.

It wasn't just Bartlett's collection of art that needed a new treatment, but also Esty's old wood dresser that was inspired by his profession for a redo. Why not cover it in linen similar to the way he would a picture frame? He and Bartlett applied textured, olive-hued linen to the dresser's surface and finished it off with vintage, distressed glass on the top and the sides.

Found objects, like a grungy paintbrush, an old wood ruler, a beat-up clock, and several chair spindles, became a museum-worthy piece of wall décor once framed inside the confines of a set of pie-shaped concrete molds. Next to them on a nearby windowsill, a nonworking, oversized

ABOVE LEFT A vintage boxing dummy hangs over lead dumbbells and framed industrial photographs.

BELOW LEFT Spindly, metal brutalist florals are arranged in a U-shaped Jonathan Adler vase in front of a Peter Dayton collage.

lightbulb found on the street has become a beautiful curiosity. "I love exposed Edison bulbs, and this one is supersized," Bartlett says. "I only wish it worked!" The collage paired with the alluring lightbulb immediately draws guests across the living room to ponder what each element once was or what it could be.

On a side table is one of Esty's pieces of portable lighting that needed a revised look for the new apartment. For their first decoupage project together, they cut out their favorite images from 1950s issues of *Holiday* magazine and glued them to the lampshade. A dramatic lighting effect was cast in the dining room with a dentist lamp from the 1920s. They replaced the original bulbs with long, tubular ones that give the piece "a more sinister effect," Bartlett says. The combined effort culminates into a

ABOVE LEFT Esty and Bartlett got crafty one evening, making this decoupage lamp shade out of photos from old *Holiday* magazines. Bartlett employed the same technique in the bathroom of his West Village men's boutique.

ABOVE RIGHT A metal cabinet made by decorator Mark Ciolli is warmed up with handmade crafts, earthy accessories, and plants.

SOFAS Esty brought along these Jean-Michel Frank–inspired sofas into his and Bartlett's eclectic living space.

LIGHTING Esty and Bartlett decoupaged the shade of an ordinary ceramic lamp (left) for a textural effect. For what Bartlett says appeals to his "sinister" sensibility, a metal articulated floor lamp (right) fits the bill.

CHAIR Richard Fasanello's Love Chair easily accommodates two and is the centerpiece of the living room

WALL ART Esty collected objects with a similar patina, such as well-used paintbrushes, a wood ruler, a few chair spindles, and a beat-up clock, to create an objet d'art within the confines of a set of terazzo molds.

contemporary, warm space, full of thought-provoking details that Bartlett calls "dark and sexy meets spiritual and subdued." This sensual, masculine emotion plays out atop a neutral palette that underscores their decorative details. "We both love neutrals, like olive and khaki, but realized we needed some color as well," Bartlett says. He leaned toward orange hues, a tendency he attributed to having spent time traveling through Thailand and Cambodia, where Bartlett marveled at the Buddhist monks wearing saffron. "Rusted metal and vintage aged colors suit both of our personalities."

ABOVE RIGHT This Edison bulb was found on the street. Even though it doesn't work, it still makes for a light-catching accessory on the windowsill.

BELOW RIGHT To create this dramatic magical hoop, decorator Mark Ciolli found a length of metal pipe snaking on the street, wrapped it in a coil, and mounted it on a block of wood.

OPPOSITE A favorite piece of art hangs next to a collection of John Derian plates and a chilling metal hook.

Frankly Speaking
Set Designer Peter Frank

For his Hudson, New York, home, set and prop designer Peter Frank has graciously accepted all the aged patinas and inconstant veins of color that peak from his decorative accents that once lived a shiny past. "My things came from all over the place, from eBay to garage sales," Frank says. "I gravitate toward things that are somewhat decrepit, but that have an interesting patina. If it's too flashy, then I'm not attracted to it." For Frank, it's a constant balancing act between texture, finish, color, and shape. But in his Hudson home, slate gray walls and deep blue grass cloth strike a masculine, modern palette for all his timeless decorative beauties.

A crisp white fireplace mantel in the living room sets a lasting impression with aged glass and vintage metals, and a repurposed door is used as a rustic mirror. The shimmer of light he created with his accessories and the decades-streaked mercury-glass mirror strike a pleasing contrast to the weathered wood that frames it. After taking home the glass, he purchased another mirror that had better reflective qualities and laminated it to the back of the old one, making it more functional while retaining the charm that attracted him in the first place. The look is elegant and authentic, with just enough rough edges to keep it from feeling overly catalog slick.

Each detail Frank adds to his home maintains a careful balance between the obviously aged and the stylized. A gold-framed display case holds a luminous set of lusterware, and an oversized sofa is an ethereal lounging spot with the help of slipcovers made of flea-market French bed linens and pillows made out of ticking scraps. For a personal touch, Frank positioned between a wall of blue grasscloth and the sofa a two-hundred-year-old

ABOVE LEFT Time-weathered mercury glass becomes a patina-rich collection.

BELOW LEFT An Edward Wormley dresser is topped with thrift-store and flea-market lighting and accessories tied together by color and shape.

OPPOSITE Frank made a slipcover from old French linens and recycled ticking fabric for accent pillows. Behind the sofa sits a two-hundred-year-old Korean screen that was passed down from his grandparents.

Korean screen of fragile paper that was passed down from his grandparents.

The subtle yet quirky thrift-store and flea-market details in Frank's home are gathered artfully into vignettes that create appealing units. In his bedroom, a curvy wood chair, an Edward Wormley chest of drawers, a framed woodcut, and a mélange of metal, wood, and ceramic objects of varied shapes and sizes all gather cohesively. "I don't really have anything of real value," Frank says. "I do have things that I've spent more money on, but pretty much I like to buy things with an interesting shape or texture." A metal-and-wood 1960s lamp he bought at a flea market fit right into the mix once he put a craft-paper shade on it. The square shade and the round base echo all the other forms around it, showing how opposing textures and finishes, when placed just right, can honestly share the same space.

ABOVE LEFT What was once a retail display case is now a framed shadow box for Frank's collection of lusterware.

ABOVE In Frank's home, rusty old hooks from a flea market make for a useful and decorative coatrack.

OPPOSITE A group of mercury glass shows glints of shine through their crackled finishes. The mirror, with much of its mercury finish flaked away, was excised from a panel of an antique door. To restore some of it reflective qualities, Frank laminated a new mirror to the back of the old one.

SHOPPING WITH SIMON: Tips from Simon Doonan, Creative Director of Barneys New York

Open up your mind for a dose of weird and a dash of the downright bizarre. Thrift shopping most certainly serves up batches of strange stuff perched among perfectly functional armoires, definitely suitable dining room chairs, and completely useful side tables. At first glance, some people might recoil when faced with a possible purchase that seems odd or unusable. However, leave it to best-selling author and Barneys New York VP/creative director Simon Doonan to dish up some, ahem, "practical" advice on how to incorporate these brow raisers right smack-dab into a truly pleasing home décor. Don't forget, however, that he's the same guy who once took toilet brushes and fashioned fabulous holiday trees to put on display at the upscale retail mecca. Embrace the eccentric oddities you might find in a thrift store. Who says you can't weave together artificial flowers for a conversation-halting piece of wall décor or paint a pair of cowboy boots gold for a pair of outlandish outdoor planters? A drop of imagination can turn a thrift-store find that prompts chuckles and gasps into an enviable home accessory.

It took our eagle-eyed shopper only a couple of minutes at Housing Works' 17th Street store to identify his first find: a silver-framed wreath of peacock feathers ($47). "I know peacock feathers are supposed to be bad luck and all, but this would look so groovy in a bathroom by itself or hanging at the end of a hallway as a focal point." The simple square frame showcases the round feather formation, making it a clean, contemporary wall accent that on closer inspection makes for a pleasing conversation piece.

Something that'll keep the Joneses yapping was exactly what Doonan found in an antique wicker baby carriage ($195). The *Rosemary's Baby* carriage, as he called it, deserved a thorough cleaning and a nice coat of nontoxic paint to transform it into a children's room hamper. "When it's full of laundry, just wheel it down the hall to the washing machine," he suggests. "And when you're done, just leave it in the hallway by your door to freak out the neighbors! Creepy!"

Wall décor is found in massive quantities at thrift stores, as Doonan witnessed on this visit. One of the best pieces he found was a high-quality,

1960s abstract oil painting ($415) that was in excellent condition. None of the paint layers was cracked and it was large enough to make a presence when displayed by itself in a room. He cautioned that this piece, with its deep orange, brown, and red circles and oblong bars, wasn't for everybody's home, as its style and color dictate what kind of décor it would fit in. Doonan says he would put it among clean, contemporary lines like those found in Danish modern furniture. "Forget it if you're all about shabby chic or Victorian curlicue kind of things," he says. "It just won't work."

Doonan's next discovery was a quartet of what appeared to be super-sized, amber cocktail glasses ($12 each). "You could be the hit of the party and invite your friends to have a glass of sherry for a laugh," he notes. But on second thought, each glass would probably hold an entire bottle in itself. From a purely decorative perspective, however, Doonan says these glass wonders of varied height make for an attractive collection on their own. Use them in the bathroom to hold guest soaps, bath salts, Q-tips, or cotton balls. Or fill them with a collection of seashells, antique buttons, plastic toy soldiers, or miniature cars. During the holidays, pack them to the rims with candies, pine cones, or potpourri. "Or you could simply plop a votive into each one," he says. "That would be delicious!"

Finally, Doonan zeroed in on two resin tusks held up on a silver-finish stand ($32) and identified them as a much sought after yet rarely tamed decorative accessory: the mantique. It's a beefy addition to a masculine setting, such as a media room, a library, a cigar room, or a teen's bedroom. The mantique adds an element of surprise no matter where it chooses to go on the prowl. "Even the most feminine of atmospheres needs at least one mantique," Doonan insists. Too much estrogen isn't good for anyone, so for a healthy balance, a mantique is de rigueur. When you bring it home, remember that it will command attention wherever you decide to place it. "As with all mantiques, this one should be treated with great respect."

ABOVE Barneys New York's Simon Doonan pushing his *Rosemary's Baby* carriage from Housing Works.

OPPOSITE, ABOVE A 1960s oil painting, perfect for a mod décor.

OPPOSITE, BELOW An example of the much revered and often misunderstood mantique.

dining and entertaining

a place at the table

Plates and saucers and glasses, oh my! Practically every thrift store is like a gigantic kitchen cupboard bursting with dining implements just begging for a new home. It's easy to see how a novice thrift shopper might find the selection vying for attention overwhelming, especially since very few examples of all this tableware seem to have anything in common: the gold-rimmed champagne flute that survived a dishwasher mishap; an incomplete set of floral plates from the '70s that felt dated when the new wedding china crowded in; or an almost-full set of silver whose owners tired of its polishing routine.

These are exactly the kinds of thrift-store finds that with a spark of imagination, some simple and clever repurposing, and an adherence to a color or a motif can establish a unique tabletop that's satisfying for everyday use and dazzling for entertaining.

Like most Americans, I never seem to have enough space in the kitchen cabinet, since buying dishes on a whim doesn't carry with it the space considerations of buying a sofa or a bed. I see a funny coffee mug at an amusement park, a stack of floral plates peering at me from a shelf, or a cut-crystal vase in a shop window, and soon enough, it's wrapped in tissue, plopped in a shopping bag, and carted on home.

Thrift-store dishes bring instant heritage and charm to a table. They mix well with the old, cozy up to the new, and add a graceful touch in composing a dining scenario that is both personalized and unforgettable. It is always possible you'll discover full sets of sought-after collectables and highly desired brand and designer names in thrift stores, but it is an absolute certainty that you'll be fascinated to the point of purchase by thrift-store tabletop goods including some dear, a few pedigreed, and others that are simply captivating or truly useful. The trick is pulling together all these mix-and-match pieces—the lonely serving platter, the tarnished silver charger, or the single martini glass—in a way that makes them look planned and not just thrown together on a table.

tell a story

Determining a color story is a practical starting point, and white dinnerware is always an appropriate and pleasing palette to build upon. Nearly every culinary creation looks appetizing on a neutral background: you never have to worry if your red sauces clash with the color of a gravy boat or if your blueberries get lost in a dark-hued bowl. Some people believe that dining off of white can trick the brain into thinking that food actually tastes better, much to the delight of many cooks, I'm sure! White is the great unifier of any dish set, as it complements all colors; it looks tasteful with clear and tinted glassware and chic with any type of flatware. Even when collected in multiple shapes, sizes, and textures, all-white dishes almost always look like they were created together, even when their origins are of a scattered nature. And finally, white is a smart foil for other dishes with fanciful trims or intricate border designs that add character to a table.

That's not to say that color should be avoided. A fudgey, chocolate cake looks even more sumptuous on the pink Melemac serving plates I found at a Kansas City thrift shop, and I love the pops of color added to a casual tabletop by the few green-and-yellow Fiestaware dessert plates from a cousin's garage sale serving as condiment holders. That said, I always consider a food's color and my dining theme before setting a table, whether it's a casual buffet or a sophisticated sit-down dinner.

BELOW Michael Quinn and Heather Kerr made this chalkboard out of a piece of discarded wood coated with Ping-Pong table paint to tally up the score between the Sweets and the Savories. The plates came from a rummage sale on Long Island.

PRECEDING PAGES An assortment of mismatched china pieces makes for a pleasing tabletop display.

use your best every day

I hardly ever delegate which dishes are for every day and which are reserved for entertaining. Instead, I tend to mix them all together liberally, and nobody would ever guess that I found the china plates for $1 or so at garage sales and thrift shops, because they coordinate quite well with casual soup bowls and salad plates from places like Crate & Barrel and Sur La Table. Every morning, I eat my yogurt and fresh fruit in an old, French porcelain café au lait bowl painted with delicate flowers. And the floral-print china serving platter that my Grandma Churchill most certainly salvaged from an estate sale is elegant enough for a candlelit dinner for two. That's not to say, however, that any dish will fit every occasion. For example, my favorite serving bowl is a greenish gray flecked Texas Ware mixing bowl I bought at a garage sale many years ago. It reminds me of the one Grandma used to stir up a creamy, yellow potato salad to serve to the hungry dinner crew alongside a gold-trimmed, estate-sale platter of pan-fried chicken, all topped off with a metal pan of crusty blackberry cobbler. For homespun meals, it makes sense that I use and serve from the bowl that reminds me of Grandma. I do think guests might find it a touch wacky if I used that beloved bowl as a champagne bucket for an elegant dinner outfitted with

ABOVE LEFT Designer Michelle Rago is a proponent of avoiding what she calls the "matchy-matchy." These drinking glasses, clearly from different sets, subtly tease the eye with their slight variations of shape and scale.

ABOVE CENTER Heather Chadduck created a collected tabletop of mismatched silver and black-and-white thift-store plates.

ABOVE RIGHT Even though these china cups don't match, Joe Maer established a unified effect by sticking to a single color palette.

OPPOSITE A guest helps himself to a cordial from a 1950s thrift-store dinette that Quinn and Kerr arranged outside their Brooklyn tailgate party.

fine china and silver. It's better saved for holding heaps of cubed ice at a beach barbecue or mounds of popcorn while watching old movies. I agree with the dining philosophy of *Cottage Living*'s Heather Chadduck, who uses a gorgeous collection of mismatched silverware every day. When it's time for cleanup, forget polishing them! Chadduck just tosses them in the dishwasher, allowing the toll of cleaning to create its own time-honored patina. She likes the varied effect in metal tones the silverware naturally takes on, adding to the vintage charm of her home.

Dining on thrift-store dishes every day makes even the simplest of meals a little more special. A bowl of tomato soup just seems to taste better in an elegant china bowl and that morning glass of OJ is even more energizing in a cut-crystal goblet.

function versus fashion

The major consideration when deciding between everyday and special-occasion dishes is really durability. Fine-bone china and porcelain, especially when they've lived a hearty past, are more fragile, chip easily, and might not hold up against the high-temperature water and harsh detergents used in a dishwasher. Always hold a prospective-purchase thrift dish up to the light to see if there are any obvious, dark veins running through the surface or any cracks in the finish, both of which might indicate overly heavy usage that'll lead to breakage in the future. Run your fingers carefully around the edges and across the surfaces to feel for any signs of unevenness that could eventually affect a piece's end use. If you're not actually going to dine on them, then display them

ABOVE Symmetry and color choice—blue and white—tie together Maer's sophisticated tea party.

ABOVE To break up the monochromatic layers of the Target martini glasses and black-and-white dishes, Joe Maer added a red burst of color with a glass flea-market vase.

within your home-design concept. However, if you are seeking true function, those little flaws may pose a hindrance.

A dishwasher can dim dishes with decorative trims, especially those of metallics. In order to preserve the current luster of ornamented dishes, they should be washed by hand. Even though it's pretty safe to say that most stone and earthenware is more attuned to today's technology, always look at the reverse of any dish to see if there are any care instructions. Products made in the late '50s began to have alerts stamped on them highlighting any special-care issues regarding washing, and many goods produced from the mid-'70s and later typically include information on microwave use. When in doubt of sturdiness, keep your thrift-store dishes out of the dishwasher and the microwave.

The fear of broken dishes can be eliminated if you choose to use melamine or plastic plates, a common find at thrift stores and garage sales, which are practically indestructible. The colors available in these materials is like dipping into a rainbow, from the palest of lavender to the rosiest of red, making these midcentury staples great for boat rides, kids' parties, or lakeside picnics. Locating good-quality examples of melamines, such as Melemac or Texas Ware, is rare; often these dishes have unsightly and unsavory scratches by the time they get to a thrift store or flea market.

in nothing flat

For flatware and serving accessories, shop for metals that are free of corrosion and have securely attached handles. Seek spoons that aren't bent and forks with tines that are straight and not all askew. Care issues, as when shopping for any other thrift-store dining goods, should also be considered. Will you be willing to wash a delicate piece by hand? Will you be bothered if you have to polish silver? Or will you toss it all right into the dishwasher? Know that if you put silver in the dishwasher, it will eventually develop more imperfections, caused by the harsh detergent and a chemical reaction with other metals in the machine. But then, that might be the effect you're looking to achieve.

Utensils with components of pearl, bone, delicate inlays, Bakelite, or wood will also require hand washing since extreme heat can cause these materials to weaken, and water that worms its way into any crevices can affect these pieces' sturdiness. For a personalized set of thrift silverware or flatware, buy patterns in even numbers to enforce a design scheme. Since it's easier to find single utensils or individual place settings than a totally coordinated, fifty-piece collection, applying the two-to-one ratio will help your flatware displays achieve the sensation of a lightly guided kismet. Start with two complete place settings of flatware that play well together, and your coordination has already begun. If each of these settings contains a matching knife, fork, salad fork, and teaspoon, then you already have eight constant design motifs that'll start to unite your flatware presentation. Sprinkle in individual pieces that play off of the color and texture of your guiding pieces, and guests will marvel at your creativity and your eclectic sense of style.

To spice up the mix, offer steak knives with varied handles, from wood and plastic to metal or horn. Or change motifs with the course. Start off the evening with your individualized silver knives and forks and swap to multicolored flatware for the festive dessert portion of the evening. The fun of buying thrift-store dinnerware is that a handful of matching pieces alongside several coordinating standouts makes for an ever-evolving dining experience—one that can be used every day or for special occasions.

art of glass

Shopping for thrift-store drinking vessels involves many of the same coordination concerns as for dishes and flatware. Overall, clear glass, whether manufactured by machine or blown and cut by hand, complements with almost any color or design. Clear glass enhances the color of a beverage, whether the bright pink of a feisty lemonade or the rich tones of a rare Burgundy. Similar to eating off of white plates, many people find it more appealing to drink cold beverages and fine wines contained in clear glass. Coordinate glasses with plates and flatware, making sure

ABOVE On one of his shopping trips searching for display items, Quinn found this plaster squirrel, which worked right into a party's theme.

FOLLOWING PAGE Let the Sweets vs. Savories competition begin! Vintage dishes, loosely arranged wildflowers, and handmade pennants set the theme for Quinn and Kerr's festive party.

they strike common chords, and always look for sets that'll enforce your design scheme throughout. Again, metallic trims, as well as printed patterns, will require special care if you want to keep them looking like the way you found them. And just like you would do with any thrift purchase, inspect items carefully. Never buy drinking glasses marred by nicks, cracks, or veins. Inspect stems on wineglasses for any hidden, tiny veins that will eventually cause the glass to snap in two.

beyond drinking

Let your imagination take you beyond the intended uses for your glasses. Serve dollops of banana pudding or chocolate mousse in champagne flutes. Fill sophisticated martini glasses with exotic granitas or summertime berries. And then there's the lone drinking glass—one that reminds you of that high school field trip to a local amusement park or your favorite Saturday-morning cartoon—that tugs so heartily at your emotions that even though it clashes with everything in your cupboards or bar area, you end up taking it right on home.

When I find that intriguing, single drinking glass, it always primes my imagination for finding uses beyond a hydrating purpose. Coordinate it with others of similar shape, color, or motif for a vignette of fanciful flower vases or multitiered votive holders. A single drinking glass may hold toothbrushes or guest soaps in your bathroom, or paintbrushes and markers in your studio. Use it in the bedroom as a catch-all to collect spare change, or as a trusted spot to stash keys, or as a handy

COLOR TIP
PARTY TIME IS THE OPPORTUNITY TO TAKE A CHANCE WITH COLOR TO SEE HOW IT AFFECTS THE TONE OF YOUR ENTERTAINING.

Just like a successful celebration has an overriding theme, color should be considered in the same way. For a tantalizing tabletop, accent colors go a long way in serving up panache within the confines of a dining experience. For a table that's dramatically set in all-white bone china and shimmering crystal and silverware, subtle color splashes will heighten the drama without detracting from the glamour that's already set before guests. Light-colored vintage linens, napkin rings, accent plates for salads and bread, and small floral arrangements can spice up any neutral-toned table setting without detracting from the main dish that'll be presented on the larger plates. For more formal affairs, such as Michelle Rago's vintage wedding (see pages 148–149), the colors are romantic and soft, accenting the serious event that just occurred.

Save dark-hued dishes—either in mysterious blacks, browns, and navies or eye-popping reds, greens, and oranges—for more casual or cocktail affairs, when dining off of large plates of food isn't the focus. Small thrift-store stoneware bread or salad plates in these dark or bright colors are excellent options for finger foods that are picked up off of a buffet and carried while mingling with other partygoers. They spread their color throughout the event, and look welcoming when stacked among the other plates and eating utensils, especially when they are of mix-and-match, coordinating colors. Colors speak and set the tone of an event. At the Quinn/Kerr tailgate party (see pages 138–143), the bright mishmash of poppy colors adds to the retro vibrancy. Vivid, intense colors say, "Pick up a banner and shout," whereas cool, quiet tones say, "Sit down, sip a rare port, and engage in quiet conversation."

holder for matchbooks. For a decorative option, fill glasses with collections of old buttons, Boy Scout badges, champagne corks, foreign coins, or scraps of colorful ribbon.

life of the party

None of my martini glasses or champagne coupes is from a complete set, but because they all share a common use and maintain a similar figure, they inherently coordinate. The same can be said for most thrift-store-curated sets of glasses, as long as their specific functions are similar. For a memorable event in your home, buy varied patterns of inexpensive glasses in similar themes—say cartoon characters, movie or historic motifs, or summertime flowers—and then invite guests to take them home as a parting gift.

Throwing a party is a perfect time to experiment with creating consistent themes and color stories with thrift-store tabletop items. Just like any decorating project, once you discover your inspiration, let your imagination spiral around the motif or color you've decided upon. When I decided to celebrate the launch of Dolly Parton's *Backwoods Barbie* album last year, my theme was right there on the CD package. Everything I chose for my tabletop and menu reflected the works of my favorite singer. My colors were pastel pinks, blues, and lavenders; my motifs were based on Dolly and Grandma's china cabinet; and, well, the signature cocktails were strong! Focus your tabletop on themes, designs, and colors, and your dining invitations will be answered with a resounding YES!

ON THE MARK
TONS OF USEFUL INFORMATION ABOUT THRIFT-STORE CHINA, PORCELAIN, OR STONEWARE DISHES IS LIKELY FOUND STAMPED ON THE REVERSE SIDE.

I always flip these dishes over out of curiosity, but I'm not really concerned with their resale value or collectability. I am amused by the countries of origin, the factories that produced them, and the special codes that often appear on more desirable pieces, but in the end, I'm looking for goods that have an appealing look, are of great quality, and are offered at an attractive price.

Unless you are a serious procurer of fine china, the cryptic code stamped on the bottom of older, more collectable dishes can be mind-boggling. You may see the manufacturer of the piece noted, the country it was made in, or the name of the pattern. Sometimes all that data is understandable, but other times it's hidden in a jumble of Roman numerals, funny symbols, and letter combinations that look more like a secret code than helpful information.

For example, identifying the manufacture dates of certain brands, such as Homer Laughlin or Wedgwood, involves knowing how a series of letters corresponds to certain months and years. Dating Worcester depends on letters and a series of dots, whereas many old Minton pieces rely on odd symbols that can range from an asterisk to an airplane. Easier to identify are labels associated with a hotel, restaurant, or cruise ship for which a specific piece was created. The oldest porcelain marks date back to the eighteenth century and the labeling continues to this date. One of the best books describing the intricacies of all these marks is *Kovels' Dictionary of Marks* by Ralph and Terry Kovel (Random House). Learning about these marks is a necessity for a serious collector, but for the casual shopper who visits thrift stores to build entertaining sets, these variables are rarely an issue.

Number Crunching
Cottage Living's *Heather Chadduck*

When does the decorating style of a home set the theme of a casual dinner party for a group of close friends? If it's at the Birmingham, Alabama, house of *Cottage Living*'s Heather Chadduck, then the concept is as easy as one, two, three—or *un, deux, trois,* considering that her love for everything French is partnered with her love for anything that can be counted.

Because her work schedule keeps her on the road, away from her charming Birmingham cottage, it's rare that Chadduck has time to throw one of her talk-of-the-neighborhood dinner parties. But when she's in town and gets the urge to entertain, she goes at it with gusto. "I don't cook very often, but when I do, I cook for eight," Chadduck says. "I love having a long seated dinner with lots of courses so that guests can settle in and hang out for a while."

Chadduck's memorable dinner events are always infused with her fascination with numbered items and center around eight chairs in her dining room that set the tone for the party. Chadduck reupholstered these flea-market and antique-auction finds with a handsome striped fabric and embroidered them with numbers, from 1 to 8. With her furniture dictating her dinner-party theme, Chadduck assembles her tabletop to reflect her

ABOVE LEFT A $35 table from a thrift store takes center stage in Chadduck's breakfast nook. She bought the now-gorgeous dining chairs at a yard sale. When she spied them, they were painted gold and had tattered striped silk seats and backs. Her Pillivuyt brasserie plates accent her collection of white ironstone and mismatched silverware.

BELOW LEFT Chadduck's English pointer, Lillie, in her favorite lounging spot on the front porch, where she can watch "for birds, squirrels, and the mailman," Chadduck says. The metal chairs, once "rusty and crusty," came from a local consignment shop. "I took them to an auto body shop, where they put on an upper hard coat of car paint, and I didn't have to deal with the sanding and painting."

OPPOSITE Everything, from the black-and-white plates and residential address numerals to the crimped French accounting ledger placemats, enforces Chadduck's fascination for anything numbered.

ABOVE Chadduck displays the back
side of a prized ironstone serving platter
by J & G Meakin by attaching
it to the wall with pieces of twine. "I
have so much that it seems to stay in
the cabinets, so I thought this was a
good opportunity to show off the
maker's mark." The wall is papered with
pages from an accounting ledger that
Chadduck found at a French flea market.

OPPOSITE Chadduck embroidered
numbers on the backs of flea-market
chairs to play up her favored motif.

counting obsession, as well as anything that has a French twist. For
drinks she selected antique reproductions from glassmaker Kiss That
Frog that have French, turn-of-the-century character but are sturdy
enough to use every day. "They're heavy, don't chip, and go right in the
dishwasher," she says. For plates, she combined Pillivuyt brasserie
reproductions and Conran's numeral-designed pieces with her own
collection of vintage white ironstone, which her father is always
keeping an eye out for when on his own antique hunts. "It's pretty
much guaranteed that either for birthdays or Christmases my dad will
give me a couple of pieces for my collection."

Her unmatched silver, which she also uses for every day, adds casual
yet sophisticated charm to the setting. "My silverware is so mismatched and half of it is tarnished, but I like it that way," she says. "I
never polish it and just throw it in the dishwasher and never worry
about it. Some of my forks are larger than the others, but that just adds
to their appeal." These mismatched silverware pieces, along with their
varied markings from old hotels, trains, and cruise ships, add a
conversational sense of discovery to a thoroughly planned table.

Pages from French accounting ledgers found at a flea market appear
at Chadduck's table as place mats with crimped edges. An old thrift-
find bucket that already had the numeral 6 stenciled on it was a must
for Chadduck. She uses it as part of a floral centerpiece.

Home-address numerals that Chadduck finds at garage sales and
thrift stores may find themselves incorporated into her tabletop as
well. "When it's somebody's birthday, I find out how old they're going
to be, buy a bottle of champagne, and attach their birthday numbers to
it," Chadduck says.

Chadduck is also known for assembling at her dinner parties groups of people who may have never dined together. So to figure out where everyone sits, she leaves it to luck and keeps a set of dice right there on the table to help decide. The numbers on the chairs and tied to the napkins correspond to the winning roll, so there's never an awkward moment when placing guests next to each other. "It's a lot of fun," she says. "You just roll the dice and you know exactly where you're going to sit."

ABOVE LEFT To air-dry her jeans across from the laundry room, Chadduck mounted a row of old hooks below botanical specimens that she pressed herself and put in thrift picture frames.

ABOVE RIGHT Chadduck turned what she believes is a numbered key box into a jewelry organizer. One of her most prized thrift possessions is the toile drapery that she saved from the garbage bin of a San Francisco hotel.

OPPOSITE In her sitting room, Chadduck mixed photos of family and friends, displaying them in frames from thrift shops. She made photocopies of the originals and printed them on photo paper in sepia and black and white. "That way, they all feel like they are from the same era," she says.

Time to Tailgate!
Best Friends Michael Quinn and Heather Kerr

Brooklynites Michael Quinn and Heather Kerr can take a theme party and roll with every detail from beginning to end. So when it came time to tackle an autumnal celebration in Quinn's 500-square-foot Carroll Gardens, Brooklyn, apartment, the idea of an indoor tailgate party seemed like a natural.

The atmospheres crafted by Quinn, a former visual director at menswear design company John Varvatos, and Kerr, a gifted jewelry designer, result in vibrant imagery that lucky invitees will remember for years to come.

For Quinn and Kerr's tailgate Super Bowl, the competition was between the Sweets and the Savories served up to guests who dressed the theme in Eisenhower jackets, plaid shirts, football jerseys, twinsets, and argyle socks. They were greeted with the sound of Tommy Dorsey Orchestra cha-chas scratching and skipping on a rickety record player, a sweet-and-spicy Dark and Stormy cocktail, and a retro spread that would make Colonel Sanders swoon. Quinn upturned a discarded door and laid out his buffet, heaped with all kinds of tailgating treats: fried chicken, baked beans, bourbon-soaked sausages, cornbread, and pickles on a stick.

Cold drinks were stashed away in old cola coolers and served up in a variety of vintage glasses. The thrift-store, pastel-tinted metal glasses

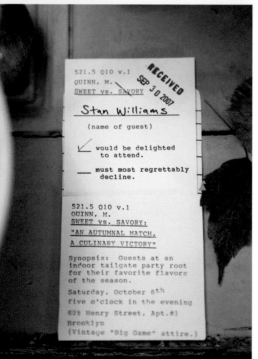

ABOVE LEFT It's time for a toast with vintage cocktail glasses.

BELOW LEFT For one of his personalized invitations, Quinn used library return cards and envelopes and manually typed out all the pertinent information for his and Kerr's Sweets vs. Savories tailgate party.

OPPOSITE, CLOCKWISE FROM TOP LEFT As the party spilled outdoors, guests could serve up shots from this herringbone cordial set. An old metal soda cooler, plaid ice buckets, and vintage thermoses keep drinks icy cold and contribute to the tailgate theme. A collegiate-inspired banner of handmade pennants drapes above the main food station. The party hosts also created felt pennants with guests' initials sewn on them, arranged them in a silver trophy, which was Quinn's first childhood thrift purchase, and offered them as a parting gift.

BAR For this collegiate tailgate party, an old vinyl and wood bar from Quinn's grandparents' house became a practical serving area.

DRINKWARE Kerr's glass pitcher from a church rummage-sale in New Jersey happened to coordinate with Quinn's metal-rimmed low-ball glasses, found at a Goodwill store in Pittsburgh.

BACKDROP A gigantic owl head that Quinn finagled out of a Henri Bendel window display keeps watch over the festive bar.

DECORATIVE ACCESSORIES Especially at festive occasions, unexpected items can add thought-provoking appeal. Here, an odd abacus lamp missing its lightbulbs and an old insulated coffee carrier promote a scholastic theme.

FLOWERS Kerr arranged the flowers with a loose hand and went for spring varietals instead of typical autumnal options. The colorful blossoms add an element of serendipity to the indoor tailgate party.

CENTERPIECE A plastic biology-class brain was picked up by one of Quinn's pals at a sidewalk sale in Manhattan's East Village. The recipe for the evening's signature cocktail, a Dark and Stormy, is typed out on a card and imbedded in one of the brain's lobes.

ABOVE LEFT Quinn typed out labels to identify beverages held in vintage containers.

ABOVE RIGHT The crafty hosts looked to Americana themes and cut and pasted them together to make individualized invitations.

OPPOSITE An autumnal tableau set the right tone for a thrift-store squirrel seemingly peering askance at the walnuts strewn about and the wax-paper bags full of sweet and savory peanuts reserved for revelers.

served double duty to also hold spring wildflowers. "In my mind, the most iconic fall flower is the mum, which I don't care for at all," Quinn says. "The colors are great, but it's too weedy looking." For all the intricate planning, Quinn adds, he wanted to inject an element of kismet to the evening. "I wanted the flowers to be wild and loose looking," he says, "like a very romanticized notion of what you would pick when you pulled up in your station wagon." Kerr arranged the flowers in casual bouquets, including ivy clipped from the back of the building to fashion tendrils of green twisting around everything.

To reinforce the Sweets vs. Savories standoff, felt pennants with appliquéd letters draped the dining room ceiling over the main buffet. Guests kept tally of their favorite food team on an old chalkboard that provided a backdrop for Quinn's collection of vintage dishes, on which diners could load up on savories and finish them off with a little something sweet. In the end, no winner was declared. But it was Quinn and Kerr's party-throwing talents that triumphed.

Polynesian Pop
Peter Moruzzi and Lauren LeBaron's LA Tiki Bar

There's nary a clue from the exterior of this midcentury house in the Silver Lake section of Los Angeles that in its basement sits a full-on tiki bar.

Once you walk through the front door of the 1949 home owned by Peter Moruzzi and his partner, Lauren LeBaron, head past the contemporary art and iconic midcentury furniture placed in the first-floor living room, and take a stairway down to what Moruzzi calls the rumpus room, you'll have traveled back in time more than fifty years, to where the tiki gods rule, the ukulele is king, and there's a mai tai in the cocktail shaker.

Having grown up in Hawaii, Moruzzi has been interested in tiki nearly his whole life. "I have always had a fondness for Polynesian pop, which was prevalent in Waikiki in the 1970s when I lived there," he says.

Even though the Polynesian hot spots commemorated by Moruzzi's tiki mugs have, for the most part, since shuttered, they live on in his grass hut, ready to fill a Zombie order or serve up a Singapore Sling.

RIGHT Even though he's never smoked a cigarette, Moruzzi has grouped a collection of Las Vegas casino ashtrays into a Brat Pack walk down memory lane.

OPPOSITE It's always cocktail time with one of Moruzzi's favorite tiki mugs, Dr. Funk, from the Hala Kahiki club just outside of Chicago.

When Moruzzi and LeBaron bought their home in Silver Lake, one of the first things Moruzzi did was turn the rumpus room into a tiki shrine.

BAR Moruzzi built a bamboo bar topped with an authentic thatched roof to accommodate his large collection of tiki memorabilia.

DRINKWARE Mugs from the most iconic tiki lounges in the country lend an authentic flair to the bar.

LIGHTING Globular resin fixtures in varied shapes, sizes, and colors add to the festive midcentury nature.

BARSTOOLS Moruzzi re-covered the seats of his bar stools to match the upholstery of his bentwood furniture in the adjacent sitting area.

DECORATIVE ACCESSORIES Match books and vintage ashtrays from tiki hot spots and the old Las Vegas strip casinos add period credibility.

ABOVE Gigantic peonies found in the dead of winter helped set the theme for Rago's romantic wedding setting.

OPPOSITE Mix-and-match china patterns create a cohesive look with their white base colors. The metallic trims bring the whole setting to life.

Theme's the Thing
Wedding and Events Designer Michelle Rago

Zeroing in on a provocative, personality-packed theme will always result in a table setting that is imaginative, inviting, and well designed, says Michelle Rago, principal of Michelle Rago, Ltd., an events-planning design firm in New York. Once you set your motif, be it a color, a shape, or even a flower, then everything should fall into place naturally.

When Rago was dreaming up a springy vintage wedding that just happened to take place in the middle of December, it was a trip to the flower market that got her creative juices flowing. Peonies caught her eye and spiraled into ideas that couldn't be stopped. "They were huge," she says, "probably eight inches across, and were the perfect floral to set in the middle of the table and accessorize throughout." She positioned the beauties in vintage candy pedestals and in an old Lenox bowl that effuses the effect of a timeless, romantic wedding. Fine china plates with delicate gold details are easily matched up with vintage, ridged milk-glass salad plates.

As enlightening as her stop by the flower market, Rago says that when incorporating vintage items into a tabletop, go into it with an open mind for using unexpected items that will create conversation among guests. One of Rago's favorite accessories is an old thirty-pound scale that was passed down from her grandfather. "I use it in so many ways," she says. "I've incorporated it into floral arrangements and put plates on it. I love it because it's not something that people would ordinarily expect to see."

The Princeton, New Jersey, native has been going to garage and tag sales since she was a child. "It was a sporting event in Princeton," Rago says. "My mom and dad would get us into the car with a coffee or a tea and we would toodle all around going to garage sales." Those garage-sale experiences, coupled with her love of flea markets and vintage shops, have throughout the years influenced her unconventional, imaginative design concepts. "Mix your glassware, mix your china, and mix your flatware. We stay away from the matchy-matchy because it's just too conventional," Rago says. "We like to combine different patterns, shapes, and textures of wonderful things so that we have a table that everyone admires."

Setting Sail—for the Birthday Boy

Everyday items, such as mass-market drinking glasses with colorful decals, might provide visual appeal to the right tabletop, just like it did when Michelle Rago set out to fashion a little boy's birthday party. "For kids, you want to have lots of color and graphics so that they'll have something to respond to." At the same time, dishes that you might not use every day, like wacky-patterned plates and mismatched table linens, might be just the spark you need to ignite conversation around the party table.

At the birthday celebration, the repurposing began when flea-market-find blue refrigerator glass turned into miniature boat hulls for a seaside transformation. The bright sailboats catch the breeze with simple dotted craft-paper sails held up by masts crafted out of ordinary, backyard-variety tree twigs. "I wanted to do something whimsical, playful, and approachable," Rago says. She mixed sturdy old ceramic plates with practically indestructible melamine soup bowls to endure any childlike behavior. And then she selected a very common thrift-store find: 1980s drinking glasses with red-striped decals on them to enhance the color palette of the table.

Again, her choice in flowers helped spread a lively, easy-breezy birthday theme across the table. Rago proudly plucked what she calls a much-maligned blossom—the common carnation. "We love carnations, and people don't realize how beautiful they can be. They are inexpensive, last a long time, and are a workhorse of a flower. You can use them as a base flower, or use the petals to provide a beautiful ambiance."

ABOVE LEFT For an added surprise, Rago placed the dotted craft paper inside dime-store compasses as a parting gift

BELOW LEFT A backyard tree twig deftly serves as a sailboat mast at this kid-friendly gathering.

OPPOSITE A color-packed nautical theme anchors childlike attention at the birthday bash. To unify her thrift tabletop that includes refrigerator glass, common pastel plates, and flame-striped drinking glasses, she brightened her theme with dotted craft-paper boat sails and zesty orange napkins and carnations.

Plated Pleasures
Prop Stylist Joe Maer

For prop stylist Joe Maer, a trip to John Derian's shop in the East Village conjured up the spirit for an afternoon tea. There, he located a natural antique fabric that had been dyed blue: the ideal building block for an elegant yet casual get-together. Next, he gathered up all shapes, sizes, and brands of blue-and-white teacups, saucers, plates, and platters regardless of their motif. His only requirement? That they have an interesting shape or pattern, and that they stay in the color family of blue and white. At this table, a handleless Japanese ceramic mug neighbors traditional teacups from France and England, all set around a 1970s West German teapot, all thrift or flea-market finds. This international potpourri of dishes, while of varied origins and motifs, is held together by his underlying blue color theme.

When creating a successful table setting, Maer suggests starting with one favorite shape, color, or texture and building from there. When abiding by a color theme, it's okay to introduce other hues into the mix, but do so carefully so as not to end up with a jumbled look that doesn't tie together. "Usually color for me is [more] important [than] textures and shapes, and styles often find unity within a color framework," Maer says. "If you find yourself unable to keep it to one or two colors, try to unify the table setting with a strong idea for each place setting." An example might be placing a twig or a flower from the same family on each plate or laying smooth river rocks next to each setting. These are just a couple of ideas that can help create a unified vision at your table.

ABOVE LEFT A succulent plant provides a no-fuss attitude at a masculine cocktail gathering. The red on the flea-market vase brightens the table.

BELOW LEFT A Piero Fornasetti serving tray with midcentury picks adds just enough shine to this dark and moody scene.

OPPOSITE For a romantic affair, Maer creates consistency with blue-and-white bowls and blue swirled glasses.

ABOVE An unusual object, such as this flea-market horse bust, can add unexpected character and drama as a centerpiece.

OPPOSITE By placing matching china sets across from each other and by mixing in varied patterns in the same color story, Maer creates a cohesive setting.

For one of Maer's masculine, urban professional cocktail parties, it was a vintage Chesterfield sofa that set the tone with its leather upholstery and buttoned-up, quilted surface. To add texture to the table, Maer placed a heavy red, white, and black glass vase he found at a flea market in San Francisco at the same table as a set of black martini glasses he found at Target. He paid careful attention to dimension, and to how different pieces would show off of others. "A clear martini glass in that situation with the black couch and the strong red vase would have disappeared," Maer says. "The black martini glasses provide an anchor to the tabletop." The manly black tone spreads to the ceramic horse head, also found at a flea market, used as a decorative accent, and the black flea-market coffee cups used for a jolt of caffeine once the cocktails shakers are put away. "The horse-head sculpture is dramatic and strong and male," he says. "It provided a forceful presence next to the rather delicate and austere coffee set." The result is a table setting that is moody and intriguing while remaining clean and unfussy. "It's a cocktail party in a bachelor pad for someone who likes design and is not afraid of bold shapes or unusual gestures," he says. "It's the urban professional, sort of James Perse meets Helmut Lang."

While putting together this affair, Maer always kept an image of that Chesterfield sofa close at hand. "When shopping, just keep that one item in mind, and a collection comes together usually easily and quickly," Maer says. Would a Piero Fornasetti harlequin-pattern serving plate found at a New York flea market fit in? Absolutely. Same goes for the wood and metal midcentury picks he selected to skewer nibblies in between sips of martinis. Just in time to toast the host!

ABOVE Reeder turned an old silver fork into a miniature easel.

OPPOSITE Transforming the everyday into the extraordinary, Reeder fashions mismatched cups and saucers into novel garden decorations.

OUT OF THE KITCHEN

Sharleen Reeder bends forks, spoons, and knives in her home-design shop, Luticia Clementine's. In her Independence, Missouri, store, she channels her creativity to work miracles with housewares that might have lapsed in luster, and gives them a shining new existence beyond their intended purposes in the kitchen.

A few years ago, the former executive secretary for a local hospital teamed up with her crafty pal Karen Finke to form a business where the two would take refurbished furniture and home goods right into people's homes and sell them, much like a Tupperware party.

About ten parties and nine months into the venture, the two realized that it was too much hard work for them to pack two vans' worth of merchandise stored in Reeder's basement and haul their goods to individual homes for the hotly anticipated decorating parties. Why not open a decorating store with a workshop upstairs so they didn't have to sand, saw, and paint in their own garages? Thus the 2003 birth of Luticia Clementine's.

Reeder's focus on one-of-a-kind, refurbished, and repurposed home goods has made her a must-stop for locals, who constantly drop in to say hello and see what wares Reeder might have discovered at a garage sale, cleaned up, and set out for sale.

What's for sure is that Reeder has added new value to the creations she makes at Luticia Clementine's. She carefully bends old forks she finds at flea markets, garage sales, and thrift stores to make picture and business card easels; and she uses cups and saucers to fashion attractive garden decorations and quaint pieces of portable lighting. Even though she also tackles simple refinishing jobs and offers design counseling in her shop, her main focus is on giving housewares a decorative or useful extension. Under Reeder's care, a china lid that's missing its tureen base is celebrated as a textured piece of wall décor or a sugar bowl that has no lid is reinvigorated as a pincushion. Reeder does admit, though, that it still pangs her to buy complete sets of dishes and silverware when she knows she is going to break them up to make individual works to sell in her store. "But I feel like if I can turn these things into something that people will actually use, then at least someone is enjoying them in their home."

sensational small spaces

make a big statement

Just because you live in a small space doesn't mean you can't
decorate it royally. Thrift-store finds are an excellent way
to either distract from the smallness of a room by making it
feel large and open or to accentuate the cozy snugness that a
space-challenged room can offer. No matter how you try to
decorate it, short of knocking out walls or building an addition,
nothing will make a living area any bigger than it already is.
So embrace your small space and focus on ways to promote its
roominess or to play up its cocooning qualities.

Small spaces require that every home furnishing be chosen with specific decorative or multitasking qualities in mind. An antique credenza originally used in a dining room might make the perfect media center, a 1970s dresser could be the exact thing you need to safe-keep important files, or a large, midcentury table might be suitable for both dining and work.

When decorating a small space, take a lifestyle inventory of your planned uses. Is your place purely for sleeping and relaxing? Then maybe creating a living area akin to a five-star hotel suite is a fine solution. Every element of this room, from its peaceful colors to a comfy bed piled high with pillows and luxurious linens, should be chosen to ensure that your resting moments are an absolute dream. In my downtown, one-bedroom apartment, I have a rosy wood Florence Knoll filing cabinet in the bedroom that serves two purposes: its sliding doors conceal a massive filing system and its surface holds a small reading lamp and a grouping of my favorite men's fragrances gathered within the confines of a silver-plated charger I found at an estate sale.

multiply the uses

Sturdy dressers and cabinets, plentiful in thrift stores, are excellent storage options. Their tops are solid display surfaces for decorative elements as well as for holding heavy electronics, such as video monitors or stereo speakers. Wardrobes or armoires don't always have to house clothes. Use them for stashing electronics and computer equipment out of view, or add interior shelves and compartments to create your own linen closet. Put a bookshelf in your kitchen for a multitiered storage solution, or turn it into an open pantry for easy access while cooking. Use a china cabinet for something other than showing off your dishes. Take it to the bedroom and display sentimental, framed photographs or a collection of colorful candlesticks in the top part, and use the base just as you would a dresser. Cabinets with doors are great for concealing clutter, which is especially dizzying when the size of a room in limited. Or, if the doors get in the way of function and the cabinet interior is

ABOVE Fred Flare's Keith Carollo and Chris Bick carry home a Japanese movie poster they found at Housing Works to brighten up the cracked bedroom walls of their 450-square-foot Manhattan apartment.

especially attractive, remove them and use the piece as a display case for a treasured collection or for creating a handy library.

Use old luggage with interesting details or logos as a side table that doubles as storage. Colorful metal or wood trays when placed on an ottoman turn into a fantastic cocktail table. Folding chairs, intended for either indoors or out, can slip away in a closet, ready to be used whenever guests arrive. A bedroom daybed when plumped with pillows and luxurious throws is an easy sofa option. (Just ask anyone who lives in a New York City studio apartment.) Even an old metal office filing cabinet doesn't have to be ugly. Paint it in a white or colorful, glossy hue to attract attention, or a matte black to let it fade into the background.

light matters

It is possible to make certain spaces appear roomier with mirrors, especially when they reflect the light from outside, enhance the theatrics of a lush floral arrangement, or focus attention on a cluster of black-and-white photos on an uncluttered wall. Reject what I call the old decorator wives' tale that might lead you to believe that a mirror always makes a room look larger. That is not always true. A cluttered room reflected in a mirror can make the space appear even more uninviting, especially if it happens to highlight an area of your home that's not worthy of framing, such as a toilet or an unattractive appliance.

A room filled with natural light, no matter the size, is always more engaging. Unless the view outside your window is a view you want to repeat on an opposing wall, resist mounting mirrors directly across. The decorative appeal seems too obvious, as if you are admitting that your room is small and you're trying too hard to increase it, and it just reflects the light right back at the source. A mirror placed to the side of a nearby window helps spread the effect further, actually broadening the perception in two directions, instead of just one.

In some instances, a large, exquisitely framed mirror is all you need to add a bit of sparkle to a tiny room. Place it behind a large sofa or lean it against an empty wall for a casual, inviting effect. Even furniture with mirrored finishes can add to this sensation. Mirrored credenzas, tabletops, and cabinet doors can spread shine throughout. When placing these pieces, ask yourself the same questions you would if they were mirrors meant to hang on the wall: What will they reflect and how will they create the illusion of room expansion?

welcome distractions

Renters typically have little control over the amount of renovation a landlord allows. Since their apartments are often small, any cracks in the walls, flaws in the ceiling, or strangely shaped rooms are much more obvious than they would be in a huge, three-story house. Thrift-store wall art can cover or distract from these defects while adding a decorative dimension to a room. Table lamps that emit sexy pools of light can move attention away from an overhead beam that seems to lower a ceiling or a stationary pole that appears to bring in the walls. They can also help guide the eye when defining specific areas within a living space. A grand chandelier can highlight a dining area and a pair of table lamps define reading or lounging areas within a living space. One thing to keep in mind when adding accessories to a room is that a consistent color story will reduce the perception of clutter.

large versus small

Scale is yet another consideration for a small space. Large-sized furniture is fine in a diminutive space when it creates visual appeal and adds to the function factor. A few large pieces make a small space feel much roomier than a bunch of smaller ones scattered everywhere. Balance your bigger pieces, such as a sofa, dining table, or credenza, with smaller pieces, such as a pair of side chairs or end tables, by working to create a pleasing symmetry and adding just enough accent to keep the room from looking as if it were stamped out by a cookie cutter. A pair of oversized, thrift-store wing chairs in coordinating upholstery could achieve enough harmony in a small room to allow a few more quirky

COLOR TIP
WHITE ISN'T YOUR ONLY OPTION WHEN TRYING TO MAKE A SMALL ROOM LOOK LARGER.

It is true that by keeping the color story of your furnishings similar to that of the walls, they will blend in easily, leaving the illusion of less clutter and more space. Deeply saturated colors on walls can make a room look grand. A neutral, sandy color can offer the feeling of depth. When choosing a color, do so by imagining how it will reduce the number of wall edges the eye perceives. A dark heather gray or chocolate brown can help cast a shadow where the walls meet, making them appear endless. But when painting a small room a dark shade, do take care when painting any moldings or trims. When you highlight those elements, you outline the shape of your room and emphasize its diminutiveness. Either paint the moldings the same color as the walls, or go a shade lighter. Another option is to paint the top moldings the color of the ceiling—if it is a shade of white, it should have a small portion of the wall color mixed in to create a healthy continuity.

additions, such as a large, 1960s abstract painting or two mismatched metal side tables. Be careful, though, to keep overstuffed chairs and sofas to a minimum as they fill up a room pretty quickly, and an over-abundance of loud patterns or colors jars the eye and creates a frantic feeling. A few large furniture pieces, such as sofas, beds, and tables, can also help delineate spaces with specific uses in mind. By placing these big pieces first and experimenting with their angles, then slowly adding smaller pieces, you'll start to discover the room's natural flow.

Maxwell Gillingham-Ryan describes flow in his book *Apartment Therapy* as being much like the way a river current moves. Anything that would block a stream of water's movement or cause it to gather and swirl creates a flow problem. The same can be said for furniture. Any piece that keeps traffic at a standstill or an arrangement that overly emphasizes one area in a room represents a restriction flow. A room should be easy to get into, but also invite curiosity and discovery. Think of it as balance. If a room looks too heavy on one end, or furniture is crammed up against all the walls, then the weight of the room is unevenly distributed throughout. Try placing large furniture pieces, such as sofas, at angles that distract from the short length of the wall. And to keep the room feeling welcoming, never block the entry view with a large piece of furniture. An evenly balanced space with lots of furniture is easier on the eye than one in which everything is stuffed into a single area.

If you live in a small space and you find a piece that you can't imagine living without, go ahead and take it home, but be prepared to make the tough decisions about your existing furniture. Do you love an armoire enough to go to the trouble of rearranging everything to accommodate it? Or are you so enamored with a 1960s loveseat that you're willing to give up a side table and chair to make room for it? Most important, know your limit. "Don't buy a side table if you already have three," says Gillingham-Ryan. With thrift furnishings, there's a tendency to overbuy because of low prices and a broad assortment. Limiting your purchases to the items you need and that fit into your design scheme will make your place, no matter how small, more functional and so much more appealing.

OPPOSITE Simonaire's loosely arranged flowers easily move from the mantel when she's working to the dinner table when she's entertaining.

Dining in the Office
Interior Designer Sharon Simonaire

Even a house that's quite large runs into challenges when it comes to creating spaces that offer dual function. But when you set off interior designer Sharon Simonaire to find function and beauty in her own 1843 three-bedroom home nestled in Sneden's Landing, just fifteen minutes away from Manhattan, the result is a room that promotes her business needs, but then easily shifts gears when it comes time for stylish entertaining.

Simonaire picked the 350-square-foot room in her 2,500-square-foot home for her work space since it received lots of sunlight from two views, exhibited a coziness with its fireplace, and was steps away from the living area, where she lounges with her daughters, Sophia and Emma, watching old movies on a Saturday night. "I wanted to have a feminine home for me and my two girls," she says. "It's a very simple house that's very easy for kids. I want to have kids over and not have them feel like they're in their parents' living room." Simonaire, who counts among her clients such celebrities as Richard Gere, Robert De Niro, and Meg Ryan, struck a heavenly deal with the Presbyterian church across the street to renovate the house. The result is a "girly," comfortable, kid-friendly home that also functions well as a place to work. Her dining/work/study efforts all center on a used Parsons table that she found at R. E. Steele Antiques in East Hampton, New York. The table elegantly offers enough comfortable seating for six at an intimate dinner, but also provides ample space to hold Simonaire's work tools: fabric swatches, paint samples, room sketches, her Mac laptop, and her Rolodex. For entertaining, Simonaire simply clears away all work evidence, tosses on a pale linen tablecloth, and tops it with scattered flowers and elegant candlesticks.

ABOVE LEFT Simonaire sticks to simple accessories on her fireplace mantel for an uncluttered yet attractive effect.

BELOW LEFT Her library is handy for research but also provides entertainment for guests who lounge in the seating area.

Her library, organized at one end of the room, is housed in a cabinet she made for a show house and serves two functions—especially important for a room with dual purposes. When she's entertaining, it allows guests to muse over a work of fiction or marvel over a design tome while sitting in the antique bobbin chair or a black Louis XIV canapé. But when it's time for Simonaire to get to work, she can consult her collection for architectural references or artistic inspiration. Across the room in a calm, sunny corner is a daybed Simonaire designed. For more table seating, Simonaire might offer a guest a bentwood Thonet chair she found at a flea market, but she prefers sitting atop one of her stools designed by Jonah Meyer, who owns Service Station in Glenford, New York. "Emma always says that she can't believe I can actually work on a three-legged stool," Simonaire says. "But it suits me. I like it. I'm comfortable. I call it the ADD stool, because I just can't sit still."

ABOVE LEFT A timeless water bottle can be used anytime, day or night.

ABOVE RIGHT When Simonaire clears off her work area, covers it with fresh linens, and sets the table, it's time to dine.

LEFT Framed pieces from well-known photographers like Herb Ritts, Frances Bacon, Paul Jasmyn, Peter Beard, and Kurt Marcus are a focal point in Simonaire's library/dining room.

OPPOSITE While she might offer a guest a seat in her bentwood Thonet chair, Simonaire prefers to work while sitting atop one of her three-legged stools made by Jonas Meyer of Serv ce Station.

A "Flare" for Fun
Fred Flare's Chris Bick and Keith Carollo

They wanted to add zip to the already zesty and carve out cute from the crafty. That's how Chris Bick and Keith Carollo, the bubbly brains behind Fred Flare, an online shop boasting "a sparkling pop presentation of our favorite things," Bick says, "from fashion, accessories, and home design to pretty much what we find ourselves obsessed with at the moment" went about prettying up their 450-square-foot, one-bedroom apartment in NYC with finds from a Housing Works store a few blocks away. The Chicago natives tapped into their combined love of visual display and knack for promotion to sass up the space they've rented for more than ten years. (In Chicago, Bick was a display designer for Urban Outfitters, and Carollo worked in the advertising department at Bloomingdale's.)

To enter Bick and Carollo's space, you first pass through a dim, 15-foot-long hallway, where outstretched arms touch both walls. This is one of those weird New York corridors common in buildings where the landlord has chopped up and reconfigured so many times over the years that you never really know where a door once lead or a wall once existed. After moving through what the duo calls their storage area, with bikes dangling from the ceiling, coats and scarves hanging from hooks, and packed boxes and bins organized on shelves, you eventually arrive in a sunspot of the bright and cheery, where a fizzy, upbeat attitude bursts in Technicolor.

Bick and Carollo's apartment appears to have been decorated by a couple of advance-placement junior high kids with an aptitude for arts and crafts, a passion for the cool and kooky, a gift for unique design, and a sense of color plucked right out of a kaleidoscope. Their furniture is light and inexpensive, and much of it came from thrift stores, was inherited from family members, or was picked up on the job. All these functional, unobtrusive pieces offer a clean palette for the whimsical art, humorous knickknacks, and decorative doodads that inhabit their space. In the kitchen awaits a delectable faux layer cake made by their pal Amy Sedaris. An assemblage of thrift-store plastic Tupperware drinking glasses turned lighting piece by their friend Tony Meredith hazily illuminates a dresser.

OPPOSITE Party girls created out of sewing notions by Patch NYC dance atop wall brackets from Urban Outfitters.

All of these objects, some original artwork and others crafted out of castoffs or acquired in a thrift-store splurge, detract from the frequently found imperfections of an old apartment such as theirs. Left unadorned, the flaws in their small space would be glaring if they were in a larger apartment. It takes a fourth or fifth look before one realizes that the ceiling above the full-sized bed in their tiny bedroom looks as if it could tumble down at any moment. Instead, the eye is more likely fascinated by the doll-like imagery on the walls, on the bed, and on the dresser. A thrift-store print of a big-eyed girl in a harlequin dress peers across the room at a series of 3-inch-tall dolls made from sewing notions by their buds at Patch NYC, known for homespun accessories and hand-finished jewelry. Across the way is a framed print by Gina Garan, who has a cult following for photographing the 1970s fashion doll Blythe.

Their fascination with everything associated with dolls and playthings directed Bick and Carollo's attention toward a drab wood dollhouse sitting under a jumble of broken light fixtures at their local Housing Works. Why not turn it into a feeding station for their two cats, Vern and Lucy? They hauled the structure home and put it in the bathtub, where it lived for three days during its transformation from a dull brown house to a clean white showpiece, complete with candy-color interior walls. The miniature rooms are decorated with mementos fit for a feline, such as decorative birds and a cat-sized minicasserole perfect for serving Vern and Lucy a special treat. If cats could read, and in the Fred Flare world they just might, their literature of choice would most certainly be the Nancy Drew novel displayed on one of the feeding station's upper floors. The old dollhouse has become not only a feeding place for their cats, but also a decorative accessory in the kitchen to show off a few of the cats' prized possessions. "They actually really seem to like it," Carollo says. "Vern's spot is blue, and Lucy's is pink, of course."

OPPOSITE Bick and Carollo turned a brown wood dollhouse they found at Housing Works into a bright feeding station for their cats.

On the Small
Interior Decorator Mark Ciolli

Mark Ciolli's lavish apartment appears to be a Park Avenue penthouse, with its Billy Baldwin slipper chairs, Maison Jansen side tables, and sophisticated accents from Sèvres and Lalique. But in actuality, Ciolli's grand living and work space is anything but large: It's a 350-square-foot walk-up studio apartment on Manhattan's once rough-and-tumble Lower East Side.

Ciolli, long and lanky with the presence of a 1940s silver-screen star, has resided in his NYC bachelor pad for the better part of two decades, taking advantage of inexpensive rent in a sizzling hot neighborhood and the opportunity to completely transform his space anytime he feels like it.

RIGHT Curated vignettes lead the eye through Ciolli's apartment. Here, a 1940s gilt-bronze mourning dove is perched next to a German bedside clock.

OPPOSITE Less isn't always better in a small space, according to Ciolli, as long as it looks collected. He chose a thrift-store silk jacquard sofa that didn't require reupholstering and a Maison Jansen gueridon that came in a set, both from Housing Works. He picked up the clock in a thrift store in Las Vegas. Below sits a Louis XV footstool that he re-covered in linen velvet.

ABOVE Ciolli installed a Murphy
bed in his 350-square-foot Lower
East Side Manhattan walk-up. It
serves double duty as a work
surface and, oh yes, a bed.

OPPOSITE When tucked away,
Ciolli's Murphy bed is hidden by a
harlequin screen he bought at
auction. It then becomes a seating
area with a Louis XVI chair from
the nineteenth century paired
with stacking tables (right) that he
bought online from Target.

Or to reimagine an object and fashion for it a completely new use or look.

The design of Ciolli's studio is successful on two fronts. He has maximized every available nook and cranny, and he's filled it with appealing objects that delight the eye and divert attention from the small space. Accessories are curated in vignettes, with a variety of shapes and sizes pulled together by a visual thread, either a color, a metallic finish, or a shared shape. Reflective surfaces, such as his silver-leafed ceiling and his carefully placed mirrors, grab sparkles of light and reflect only attractive room accents. Not a subscriber to the idea of less is more, Ciolli has glorified a home that boldly mixes fine antiques and vintage collectables with thrift-store finds and a smattering of new items as well.

From broken pieces of mercury glass, Ciolli crafted a provocative fireplace mantel. "Wherever I see broken mercury glass somewhere, I save it and use it for projects like this, or for cutting down into smaller mirrors," Ciolli says. Other re-creations he displays include keyboard supports that Ciolli salvaged from a Victorian piano and turned into lamps. They sit on either side of a Louis Philippe—style chest of drawers that he had lacquered in black and uses as a media unit. The wonder continues with a valuable Louis XVI chair that sits next to a simple pair of stacking tables from Target. A few feet away he's perched a 1940s gilt-bronze mourning dove alongside a German bedside clock that he bought for $1. Two Maison Jansen side tables sit among the thrift treasures and impressive antiques in his living area. Ciolli discovered the 1970s gueridons supporting a gigantic, yet unimpressive, piece of glass hidden among the stacks of furniture at a local Housing Works. For $45, he adopted the two pieces, knowing that they were worth at least $1,000 apiece, and topped them with individual marble slabs for two tables more appropriate for his tiny space. Ciolli has mixed the precious with the penny-wise for a space that looks like a spectacular sitting room fit for an Astor or a Vanderbilt instead of a decorator residing in a studio apartment.

The decorative elements spread to a colorful harlequin screen that Ciolli bought at a Bill Doyle auction and that now serves as a trifold door for the cabinet that houses his Murphy bed. To keep track of his work files, he delegates each of his client's records to a vintage handbag. They've become natural-looking accents within the design scheme, sitting by a chair, tucked under a table, or maybe left on the dresser, as if waiting to be picked up by some well-heeled patron. They are a humorous yet practical element to his glamorous apartment that enables him to organize clients' fabric swatches, drawings, and specifications. And they're ready to go when Ciolli dashes out the door to shop for a chandelier or examine paint chips and carpet samples.

In this New York space, a tuxedo sofa acquired from Housing Works has endured at least two bouts of redecorating. For Ciolli, it was a perfect find: the gold-and-white jacquard upholstery was in pristine condition, so he kept it the way it was. The price was right at $245, and it measured 110 inches long—perfect for lounging his 6-foot, 1-inch frame. For a split second, he considered moving it to his Fort Lauderdale home, but realized that it wouldn't fit out the front door since his most recent redo diminished the space that allowed the sofa to pass through in the first place. So for now, it serves as a necessary element for Ciolli's comfort. "I love it because it's the first sofa that I can actually sleep on if I want to."

When it comes to entertaining, Ciolli isn't sheepish about having large groups over, even though he worries about too many feet trampling his white Berber carpeting. But only for a fleeting moment. Even with all the splendor he has created in his small space, he'd still rather enjoy it to the hilt than tiptoe around it like in a museum. "I can seat twelve people comfortably for a cocktail party," Ciolli says. "And I still have room to walk through the room with a tray full of martinis!"

ABOVE Ciolli made his own mantel of mirrored glass and decorated it with items that were found at thrift stores and antiques shops. On top, a nineteenth-century Sèvres fruit cooler is displayed proudly with eighteenth-century Venetian candlesticks.

OPPOSITE On Ciolli's media center are lamps he made from Victorian piano supports. The pair is atop a Louis Philippe–style chest of drawers that he lacquered in black to suit the style of his apartment. Above the Louis XVI chair hangs a French print of Heracles that he mounted within two frames from two flea markets for a grand total of $10.

LESS IS MAER: Prop Stylist Joe Maer Fashioned His 400-Square-Foot Apartment After a Minimal and Functional Downtown Boutique Hotel Suite.

A former architect whose clientele now includes Crate & Barrel, West Elm, and Williams-Sonoma, Joe Maer has tapped into his years of visual merchandising experience to create a New York crash pad with items found almost exclusively at flea markets and thrift stores. His own living space offers several examples of creating a chic, uncluttered space that also maintains a visual edge.

- Limit the large. Oversized upholstered pieces and big wooden furniture won't be found in Maer's small space. Since creating a restful environment was the goal, too many pieces would detract from the peacefulness. The only large element in this room is Maer's bed, which he draped with a turn-of-the-century cover he found at a flea market.

- Repurpose for function. Next to his bed sits a Danish modern stool from a New York flea market that serves as a side table. At $100, it was a bargain for Maer, and the height of the stool makes it perfect for a nightstand. For bedside reading, he illuminates a black metal Thomas O'Brien reading lamp from Target.

- Create cohesive vignettes. Maer selected a variety of white glass of different shapes and textures to create an appealing vignette. Sticking to one color makes the effect look planned, whereas the different shapes and sizes offer whimsy and spark imagination. "White glass is something that I collect," Maer says. "Some of it is valuable, and some of it is not. It's all about the shape and color."

- Lean wall décor. By not permanently fixing art pieces to the wall, Maer created a sense of lightness to the room. The angles at which they tilt, whether against the wall or atop a Parsons table, give his framed pieces a feeling of being alive. And since they can easily be moved from place to place, it makes it easier to change the look of his small space when he feels the urge to switch things around. "When I'm home, I am always changing things," Maer says. "I always like to move things and rearrange."

escapes

decorate a distinct getaway

The best thing about a personal escape is that it can be anyplace you decide to make it. It can be thousands of miles away, on the opposite end of the earth, or located nearby, across the street or in a nook in your urban apartment. You can relegate it to the corner of your office or spread it out across an entire floor of your home. Even though these places vary wildly in location and size, the one commonality they maintain is their dedication to the moments you'll savor for yourself or the distance they give you from all the distracting little things in life—the things that make you look around and say, for instance, "Oh, I need to straighten up that pile of magazines or pay those bills."

ABOVE LEFT Simple pleasures, like working a jigsaw puzzle and sipping a glass of wine, help the mind wander away from everyday hassles.

ABOVE RIGHT Wicker furniture sets a relaxing tone in a beach cottage on Saltaire, Long Island.

PREVIOUS PAGES A serene moment at designer James "Ford" Huniford's boat house on Fairyland Island.

These carved-out niches are places of comfort and respite—where thrift furnishings that have lived a healthy existence bring with them a similar sensation of rediscovering a long-lost friend, one who's familiar to your psyche yet, over time, slightly changed in appearance. These furnishings are packed with emotion, sentiment, and lingering memories that are hardly ever forgotten. Used pieces of furniture, proudly displaying their scratches, dings, and imperfections, have already lost any pretensions that they may have harbored when brand-new. Their sheen has been softened with age, allowing them to ease into a décor without screaming for attention.

In sparse, clean settings crafted to produce a Zen state of mind, time-honored furniture and accessories with quiet finishes and washed-out colors can soothe. Simple wooden modern designs with neutral-colored upholstery and earthy decorative accessories can maintain a soft palette that doesn't distract from any deep concentration or meditative activities. Natural elements, such as bamboo motifs, wood grains, warm

pottery, and burnished metals, can give the sensation of bringing the outside indoors. Even on the coldest of days, warming elements from the outdoors will shift the impression toward the bright and sunny.

seeking comfort

Thrift furniture can also deliver a sense of familiarity and luxury that promotes nesting and lounging. Deep-seated, plush upholstered chairs; substantial wood tables; and dark shelving make a cozy reading spot. An ordinary bedroom becomes a boudoir with high-quality, twentieth-century reproductions of French and Italian antiques from thrift stores. The corner of a family room can accommodate a meditation area or a personal shrine, lit by votives dropped in coordinating, flea-market candleholders. Even a thrift-store-cultivated collection can transport you from desk work. Photos of your favorite people mounted inside used picture frames can be set up in almost any small space. Paint all the

ABOVE LEFT An unadorned iron-stone compote and Swedish pitcher sit next to hand-blown Murano glass candlesticks on a simple wood chest.

ABOVE RIGHT A no-longer-used clawfoot bathtub becomes clever storage for beach towels.

frames the same color for cohesiveness, and you'll have a decorative unit that can travel if you want it to.

Even if they are frayed around the edges or retain scruffily charming finishes, personal escapes almost always spark emotion, whether they're chosen for their possibilities of peaceful sensation, bursts of creativity, or soul-searching. When I surround myself with objects that hold a legacy of the past, I'm always happier and feel more centered.

During the summer, my trusted getaway is aboard *The Luxor,* a 1966 wooden Chris Craft boat I share with a tight-knit group of friends. During the winter, *The Luxor* calls Sayville, Long Island, her home base, but when the warm weather starts to approach, she is ready for her forty-five-minute voyage across the Great South Bay to the Fire Island harbor where she docks during the summer and early-autumn months. As I prepare the old boat for its annual summer season, I'm energized with the anticipation of long, warm days, filled with catnaps, good books, great food, and friends. Each spring, I survey the contents of the 44-foot vessel we call our summer home and start putting together bedding combinations that almost match, sort and toss out silverware that has corroded or rusted over the winter, wipe away winter grime from the deck furniture and dishes, and then get to work polishing the mahogany finishes that have endured more than forty years of sea water, hot sun, and moist air. Most of the bath towels, embroidered with jaunty nautical motifs, have been on *The Luxor* for more than twenty years. The banquettes at the dinette shift under your seat, sometimes making for uncomfortable positions at mealtime. But what we have there belongs to the boat, and each season we feel privileged to use these items once again. Life there is unfussy, and we never worry about a plate that breaks or a deck chair that cracks under the weight of an unsuspecting guest. We hardly fuss about decorating our boat, as we let her vintage grace age with charm and dignity.

Maintaining a boat at a popular summer resort sounds to many like a life of glamorous excess. Friends are always amazed when I tell them where I laze over the summer months. They imagine a jet-set, paparazzi-packed harbor scene populated by expensive yachts and the rich glitterati

ABOVE An old wood table is brightened up with a coat of white paint and a floral design stenciled on it surface.

OPPOSITE The Go-Go's Jane Wiedlin was attracted to her Little Tokyo loft in downtown LA because of its sun-drenched skyscraper views.

FOLLOWING PAGE Old street signs and found antlers become thought-provoking details in the sunroom of the Beqaj residence on Saltaire.

who inhabit them. That notion couldn't be farther from my reality. *The Luxor* is nothing like Aristotle Onassis's *Christina,* with its whale skin–covered bar stools and multiple cabins tended to at all hours of the day by a full staff. About the only similarities between these two boats is that they both float and they both have served for years as prized getaways for the people who have always cherished them.

Nothing compares to the sounds of a wood boat rocking soulfully in the moonlit water. The lines creak against the tension of the waves and the water delicately rolls and tumbles against its hull. The gentle movement eases one's mind as you notice the chirping frogs in the woods and savor a moment you know won't last forever. Maybe that's why we hold on to every moment we spend on *The Luxor*—even the ones that have us scrutinizing about how to make a toilet flush or fix a leaky window—for ultimately, we know her fragility will eventually give into the elements that will bring about her demise.

Personal spaces are fragile, not meant to exist forever. But in memory, you can travel to them anytime you please.

COLOR TIP
COLORS CAN INSPIRE US, WAKE US FROM OUR WINTER SLUMBER, OR PUT US AT EASE WHEN THE WHIR AND WHINE OF TODAY'S WORLD IS ABOUT TO LEAVE US SHORT-WIRED.

The way you add color to a room, whether you're considering a cozy reading nook or a bright, spacious beach house, will make all the difference to the room's success as an escape from your humdrum daily routine.

Thrift-store purchases enable you to experiment with favorite colors, since the investment is small and the effect can be powerful. If you're designing around a bold color that you just can't seem to get enough of, choose two subtle accent colors that'll complement your first hue. White walls will accommodate a broader variety of color in your decorating plans. Take care, however, that your colors mesh with one another, since starkness of the walls will only highlight a mishmash of all your colored thrift finds. If this space is meant to promote serenity and peacefulness, the look of a cluttered junk shop is probably not what you're going after. Collections in relaxing colors—eggshell blues, pale greens, and clean whites—can offer interest in shape, quantity, and texture without being visually alarming. Bright colors—zesty oranges, primary reds, lush greens, and vivid yellows—excite an interior, and guide the eye through a background of neutral furniture placed among unobtrusive wall tones. Intricate designs of primary colors on thrift-store quilts or eye-catching geometric prints can move the perspective from one point to another.

Dark colors amplify the sexiness and snugness of a room. Rich walls, in chocolate brown, Moroccan red, or even the darkest of grays, set a seductive background for thrift furniture that is finished in a deep, natural stain or simply painted in intense shades. Clear glass and metallic accessories add shine without diminishing the drama of these deep hues. Thrift-store mirrors are one of the most creative and flexible purchases for enforcing and enhancing a color theme in a personal escape. The reflective quality will either enhance the brightness of the room or add subtle shimmer to whatever surrounds it. Paint the frame in a tone that will complement the wall color, either to stand out in an invigorating setting or to fade into a more mysterious background.

A Beach Hideaway
A Vintage Life on Saltaire

It must be high noon on Saltaire when the moan of a siren jolts one from a snooze on the beach and ruffles the wings of the fluttering monarchs on a sunny day. The bellowing bounces across neighboring communities dotting Fire Island, a fragile sliver of landmass that runs parallel to New York's Long Island. It's time to start thinking about getting to the tennis courts for a neighborly match, or about kicking up the barbecue.

For folks residing in this family-oriented community with miles of boardwalks, the most popular mode of transportation, next to hoofing it, is a trusty bicycle—usually one that's rusty and dented, since its lifespan is one spent in the elements and a replacement doesn't come until it completely falls apart. The only way to get onto the island is to hop a ferry across the Great South Bay from Bay Shore. Depending on the schedule, the boat sometimes stops at nearby Kismet before it reaches the destination of Saltaire, where five o'clock signals cocktail hour.

Friends and neighbors still congregate on porches filled with old wicker furniture, jars of sea glass, and lamps covered with crafty lamp shades made by a local artisan. Just like the provisions that travel from the mainland via boat, so too do all home furnishings. That's why the scuffed and paint-layered beds, dented and dinged dressers, and chipped ginger-jar lamps that inhabit these old cottages have, for the most part, been there for years. The salt air and the ocean humidity have added a decorative dimension to these items, creating an esteemed, weather-worn patina much like that of items found in thrift stores. Shiny, brand-new furniture

ABOVE LEFT Weathered antlers and bones add a touch of nature to the glass bottles and porcelains on the sun porch in the Beqaj cottage.

BELOW LEFT A wicker swing from a Vanderbilt estate went from a front porch to another home's breakfast nook to serve as an innovative seating solution.

OPPOSITE Prop stylist Mary-Ellen Weinrib bought these brightly colored chairs at Housing Works and brought them across the bay to her beach cottage on Saltaire.

BED In places like Saltaire, wood beds such as this one from the 1930s tend to stay put in the houses they were intended for.

LINENS The red bed linens and pillows add a bright spot in a room that is relaxing and casual.

LIGHTING To accommodate bedside reading, a simple table lamp is small enough to move from room to room.

SIDE CHAIR A midcentury wooden chair serves double duty; it can be used for seating or as a bedside table. Even though it's of a different period from the bed, it looks right at home in this bedroom.

CURTAINS Simple lace panels hung in front of the windows allow sunlight in and keep with the casual atmosphere of life on Saltaire.

ABOVE LEFT A nautical theme in a boy's room complements the atmosphere on Saltaire.

ABOVE RIGHT A collection of mugs celebrating Great Britain's royalty is on display on the windowsill. "The first one I had was from Queen Elizabeth's jubilee and it was given as a gift," Ali Beqaj says. Now it's become a collection that friends like to add to.

OPPOSITE A 1960s printed tablecloth that cost $2 at a thrift store brightens up an afternoon cake-and-tea party.

would look jarring in this casual atmosphere, whereas goods that have been tapped by history and seasoned by time are welcoming.

On Saltaire, an aged wood table might get a slight face-lift with floral stenciling on its surface, or a group of wood chairs whose shapes have absolutely nothing in common may become a set when painted in complementary colors. A pair of metal twin beds very well might have provided a good night's sleep in a house since it was built. Their finish has degraded with age, making them even more appealing in their delightfully dilapidated surroundings. If one needs a new porch swing, a neighbor might have one that'll do the trick.

Former *House Beautiful* editor and prop stylist Mary-Ellen Weinrib has called Saltaire her summer home for decades. She's accustomed to coordinating mismatched sets of dishes for a charming dinner party or slapping a coat of paint on a chair, even when she knows it will probably peel off by

season's end. When she does bring something over from the mainland, it must be something easily packed in a box or that stacks into a manageable form, like the colorful contemporary chairs she located at a Housing Works thrift store to enliven her simple wood dining table, which has dutifully served for many years.

Repurposing takes a strong hold when decorating in this casual beach community. An unused claw-foot bathtub might become handy towel storage, or a set of clear fish bowls might turn into display vessels for treasured collections, which tend to be accumulated from the sandy beach: sea glass, sea shells, driftwood, or horns. Dinnerware tends to be of the mix-and-match variety. Solid teacups mix heartily with beach-themed mugs, and sets of silver tarnish practically overnight. In Carolyn and Ali Beqaj's home, a set of mugs celebrating Britain's royalty grows every season at its place of honor above the kitchen sink. Ali's first acquisition portrayed Queen Elizabeth's jubilee, and has been expanded upon as guests add to the humorous grouping. His young daughter recently added a mug to his collection—one that she found in a thrift store in the UK.

With the exception of today's electronic technology, hardly anything is new on Saltaire. The houses have aged gracefully in this beach community, along with their contents, which usually stay right where they are until their final moments. With each wave that nips the sandy beach on a shortened fall day, and every barn swallow that stops by on its way south for the winter, life continues on Saltaire much as it has for the last century.

ABOVE Collected trophies, boat models, and award plaques convey a nautical theme.

OPPOSITE Chairs of varying shapes and sizes become a pleasing set when painted in a red, white, and green color story.

A Place for Peace
Hardware Sculptor Carl Martinez

New York hardware sculptor Carl Martinez dreamed of a different life—one that recaptured childhood memories and brought him closer to the way he lived many years ago. So when the opportunity came for him to live closer to his parents, he simply moved them right in with him. Martinez, who spends part of his time working in Manhattan, escapes from the city to his turn-of-the-century mansion in Easton, Pennsylvania, where his travel-loving parents now live full-time.

Born in Washington, D.C., to an American father and an Iranian mother, Martinez moved back to Iran soon after his birth and spent the next seventeen years there. When the revolution broke out in 1979, the family returned to the States. Although Iran is now a nation in tumult, Martinez says that it was, in fact, a pleasant place for a child to grow up. His sunny memories are filled with images of running freely through the bazaars, drinking tea in lush gardens, and listening to poetry. "We always used our backyard," he says. "Nearly all of our activities were focused on being outdoors."

It was the access to flora and fauna and the appealing sense of community in Easton that transfixed Martinez. On one of his frequent visits to friends who already lived there, he was struck with a realization: He wanted to change his living environment. He pined for a serene setting to live in. He was frazzled by the ups and downs of the city, and he felt cramped in his small apartment. He needed to stretch out. "I got to the point in my life where I had lived in New York for twenty years, sort of like a transient person renting and moving from place to place, and I really wanted to own something," he says. "I wanted it to be a place like Mayberry," he says, "where you actually talk to the postman. I really like nature, and that's why I found Easton so appealing. It sort of reminds me of a place in an Edward Hopper painting, and you don't see too many places like that anymore. It's a place where I can collect rocks. I can swim in the Delaware River. I can bring home stray cats. I can collect bits of nature that inspire my work."

ABOVE A display case becomes a table next to a reproduction Louis XV chair that Martinez found in a junk shop. He even incorporated a piece of bamboo, which he normally employs to remove leaves from his gutter, into his décor.

OPPOSITE, LEFT Earthy elements and aged finishes accent the library.

OPPOSITE, RIGHT An American cloche on a chest covers a bunch of glass grapes that came from a Turkish light fixture. Behind it leans a panel from an old stained-glass skylight. The glass orbs on the floor and the leaning neon light project an airy quality next to a finial "that weighs a ton," which Martinez salvaged from a brownstone.

So for his warm and welcoming Easton getaway, Martinez mixes his thrift finds carefully with the natural elements he includes in every room. "I like the beauty of a stark room," he says, but it's the earthiness he promotes that keeps a room from becoming sterile and cold. A pair of metal-and-wood school chairs basks in the sun across the way from a chunk of driftwood rested in a corner. Lightly sprinkled dashes of Persian glasses and accessories live in a half-stripped cabinet that appears naturally weathered and beaten down with age.

Martinez's touch of nature might appear in another piece of driftwood that he recovered from the Delaware River, a rock that he kicked up on a long walk, or in some wild grasses that brushed against his legs on a wooded trail, prompting him to carry them home and display them in a vase. "I always tell my friends that if they want to get me a gift, they should just send me a rock," Martinez says. "I don't want Gucci or Prada."

ABOVE LEFT A pestle and mortar used to grind saffron sit among the glass and pottery that remind Martinez of growing up in Iran.

BELOW LEFT Rather than hang the turn-of-the-century mirror, Martinez reveals his true nature by casually resting it against the wall.

OPPOSITE One decorative accessory Martinez chose to mount is a wood and glass display shelf that he likes to keep absolutely empty.

One of the very few items Martinez has bothered to mount on a wall with a hammer and nail is a tiny glass cabinet in his bedroom. "I don't like to see tons of things hanging around, except in my work area," he says. "I love things that lean. I don't gravitate to things that hang, and when you don't hang things, you can move them easily." Instead of using the cabinet for the intended purpose of showing off objects, Martinez has left the case completely empty. There's not one dish or bowl inside. Much like Martinez, it, too, has a refreshed attitude. Rather than serving a function of displaying other objects, it stands alone to serve as a decorative piece; much of the clutter from a past life has disappeared, and lightness revives the new one.

ABOVE LEFT Martinez employs a thrift-store dresser and a metal locker "that has a classic clinic appearance" in a room his brother uses on his visits to the Easton home.

ABOVE RIGHT Elements of nature, such as leaves of wild grass, appear throughout the home.

OPPOSITE Unlike the rest of his house, the inspiration board bursts with shapes and colors. The Bakelite clock is one of Martinez's favorite things. "It's a loud clock and I like it," he says. "I like hearing it, not ticking, but this loud motor running."

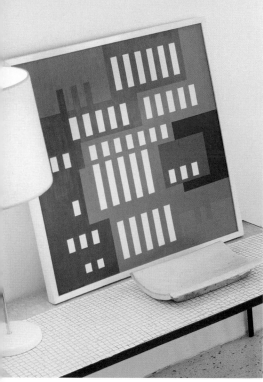

Palm Springs for the Asking
GQ's *Jim Moore*

When you want something badly enough, you feel it in your gut so strongly that there's absolutely no question the desire is going to become a reality. That's how Jim Moore, *GQ*'s creative director, felt when he began house shopping in Palm Springs. During the '80s, Moore started bringing his entire family from chilly Saint Paul to spend the winter holidays in the warm desert community. They stayed in a rental house, celebrating the season by taking dips in the pool, strolling around town in the bright sunlight, playing games, and thrift-store shopping. But in the early '90s, Moore decided it was time to buy and focused his efforts on seven experimental steel-frame houses designed by Donald Wexler in the '60s.

Of all the houses he was shown, the one he wanted didn't have a FOR SALE sign on it. "Can't you just knock on the door to find out?" Moore thought. And that's just what he did. As luck would have it, the woman who answered the door, and who is Moore's current Palm Springs caretaker, was quick to inform him that, yes, in fact, her son would probably part with the house. One might wonder what attracted Moore, a man known internationally for his sense of style, to a property that had an enclosed Mediterranean-style garage on a dirt driveway, a pool surrounded by overgrown grass, purple Mylar on the windows, and old shag carpeting on the floors. Moore, however, sensed that all this unappealing artifice was hiding something worth pursuing. And his intuition was absolutely spot on. He was amazed to find under that nasty floor covering gorgeous terrazzo floors, while neighboring houses had floors that were poured concrete. The other Wexlers had aluminum door frames, while the ones in Moore's house were made of steel.

Once Moore set to decorating his new home, he admits making a few mistakes by selecting furniture that was too large for the small scale of the rooms. He quickly rectified the mistake by tapping into the original DNA of the home. "I didn't want it to be too kooky or too precious, so I decided to honor the architecture of the neighborhood," he said. He happily undertook his mission by visiting local flea markets and thrift stores to

LEFT Moore found this piece of Arch Pottery heaped with junk at a local thrift store and it wasn't even for sale. Once again, he negotiated a great price: $40.

OPPOSITE, ABOVE Easy-on-the-eye butterfly chairs scattered around the outside of Moore's Palm Springs Wexler home offer a casual invitation to guests.

OPPOSITE, BELOW A painting from a local artist sits atop a mosaic and metal table Moore spotted at a Parisian flea market. "When I see something I love, I buy it, and then deal with how I'm going to get it here," he says. For the table's transcontinental flight, he had the legs removed from the base, and then had them welded back on when he arrived in Palm Springs. "It's an artisan piece from the late '50s," he says. "I was dazzled by its sophisticated colors and primitive craftsmanship."

BED In an unassuming modern room, a simple bed frame without a headboard invites rest and relaxation.

LAMPS A pair of wicker and metal lamps from a Parisian antiques store sits well with all of Moore's other thrift-store finds.

NIGHTSTANDS These midcentury deeply grained wood side tables only set Moore back $25 apiece at a Palm Springs thrift shop.

PILLOW A Jonathan Adler geometric pillow accentuates the oval shapes of the bedside lamps and adds a bold pop of color.

CHAIR A midcentury seat from a local thrift store retains the heritage of the 1960s Donald Wexler home.

take his pick of midcentury furniture and modern art pieces, mixing them comfortably with other finds that he procured from his travels around the world.

On a tour of Moore's house, he is apt to point out what was sold to him in a Paris antiques store: one-of-a-kind wicker and metal lighting fixtures recently knocked off by a mass retailer. The French lighting sits atop deeply grained wood side tables that Moore paid $25 for at a local thrift store. His dining room is a testament to the art of thrift shopping. The simple, contemporary, nonpedigree wood table he paid next to nothing for is matched with a set of molded plastic Eames chairs, all from local thrift shops. And then there's the gigantic piece of Arch Pottery, which to the unobservant shopping eye could have easily been passed over. "I saw it in the corner of a thrift store with a NOT FOR SALE sign on it, and it was piled with junk," Moore says. Again, he asked the shopkeeper what he wanted for the piece, but the keeper was reluctant to clean out the heap of merchandise that filled the vessel. Moore persisted, until the keeper finally responded, "Oh, okay, why don't you give me forty bucks for it."

Moore took home a spectacular geometric painting that he saw being dropped off in a truck at another of his favorite Palm Springs thrift haunts. He was prepared to part with up to $2,000 for the artwork, so he asked the man what he wanted for it. The response Moore got stunned him: "He told me that it was a really good piece and that it was going to cost me at least $200," he said. He quickly shelled out the cash and carted it home, where it has captured the attention of his impressive roster of houseguests. Savile Row tailor Richard James was so taken with the piece he used it for the basis of a tie design, even though the original artist remains unknown.

Moore relishes the tranquility of his Palm Springs home, worlds away from the fashion hubbub of New York City, where he works, and the

ABOVE LEFT The geometric painting Moore literally bought off the back of a truck.

ABOVE RIGHT A span of mountains and sky from the living room, which has played host to ad campaigns for Gucci, Guess Jeans, and Target. At left, a ceramic lamp with a cutout base that Moore paid $10 for at a thrift store in neighboring Cathedral City.

OPPOSITE A midcentury wicker saucer chair sits next to an unobtrusive white console that invites guests to peruse Moore's selection of fashion, art, and design books.

edginess of Williamsburg, Brooklyn, where he lives in the top floors of a brownstone. While Moore is monitoring his BlackBerry on the white sectional in his sun-filled living room, his demanding work schedule seems less strenuous to him as he gazes out at the shimmering pool, highlighted by a massive expanse of desert skyline. "I love being here so much that even when I'm working, it's not like working," he says. "I don't care if it's just a long weekend; anytime I can come here, I just do it." It's a break from his hectic schedule, one that immediately calms and rejuvenates. Moore treasures his home away from home as the sanctuary he is thankful to have claimed. All he had to do was ask.

ABOVE In the dressing room, Jonamor Décor combined the Asian theme with inexpensive thrift pieces.

Space Invaders
The Go-Go's Jane Wiedlin

One of Jane Wiedlin's worst nightmares has her living in a beige tract house that looks like every other one in the neighborhood. "I will always choose the less practical but more interesting choice over the sensible one," says Wiedlin, a musician, songwriter, and member of the '80s rock band the Go-Go's. "I've never had the slightest tendency toward what most people think is 'good taste' in decorating." By culling creative collections out of an affinity for girly-girl barware, accenting her adoration of sci-fi memorabilia, flexing a passion for the futuristic, and playing up a panoramic view of downtown LA, Wiedlin has turned a part-time living loft into a tasty tour stop. Originally purchased as a primary living space, Wiedlin's Little Tokyo apartment has for the most part become her secondary residence, since these days she spends much of her time living and working in Madison, Wisconsin.

A self-described gypsy, Wiedlin has bought and sold at least ten houses in the past twenty years. "Every home I've ever owned has dictated its style to me," she says. "But one thing is always consistent: I cherish character and individuality above all else." So it's no surprise that on this real-estate acquisition, Wiedlin's design influence seemed to flow right through the massive expanse of windows that open upon towering skyscrapers and a metropolitan cityscape. "The loft itself was very industrial, and in Little Tokyo, it was easy to get inspired to create a science-fiction/Asian/vintage/high-tech look."

Wiedlin lifted snippets from films like *Blade Runner, A Clockwork Orange,* and *Barbarella,* and linked them into space-aged childhood memories to make a personal retreat that has the feeling of a gigantic playroom dedicated to all the things she loves. For Wiedlin, it's the perfect place to reenergize her creativity and cocoon herself in fond memories of the past. One corner near the stairway leading to her sleeping loft is dedicated to *Star Trek* and *Star Wars* memorabilia. "I've been a huge sci-fi fan since I was a little kid, and my family all used to love watching the original *Star Trek,*" she says. "Of course, I fell in love with *Star Wars* when it came out."

To satisfy her fascination with retro pinup girls—an image that Wiedlin enjoys emulating and accumulating—she gathered burlesque-inspired barware and grouped it on rows of metal shelves encircling a silver-painted column that serves as a backdrop for the singular, visual centerpiece. Then for the Asian twist, a Chinese-inspired wood-and-glass-flecked dragon discovered in a local antiques shop adorns her dressing room, paired with another fire-breathing beast, this time a metal, gilded creature holding a light fixture shaped like a bunch of multicolored grapes—a thrift discovery made while shopping online.

ABOVE LEFT Jonamor Décor went for lots of futuristic shine in the LA loft.

ABOVE RIGHT Wiedlin says that one of her best vintage finds was this futuristic JVC Videosphere television that just happens to be orange, a color that Jonona Amor slipped into the color scheme, even though Wiedlin at first didn't care for it. "I finally gave in to the orange! Now I love it, especially pairing it with red and/or silver."

OPPOSITE Wiedlin went for a "future rustic" effect on the fireplace with stones and glitter grout by LA's Skellramics. On the mantel are her prized ceramics by Dorothy Kindell.

PRECEDING PAGES, LEFT The turning point for Wiedlin's perceived dislike of the color orange was the discovery of reflective wallpaper used on the set of *Barbarella*. RIGHT Her collection of memorabilia from *Star Trek* and *Star Wars* evokes fond childhood memories.

While Wiedlin is accustomed to decorating her homes single-handedly, this time she reached out to Jonamor Décor's Senor and Jonona Amor for help. She met the design team when they hosted a vintage wallpaper party in their Hollywood design studio and art gallery, Retropia. "It sounded so fun and silly, but interesting, too," Wiedlin says. "I met Senor and Jonona that night, and we hit it off immediately. When I told them I wanted to do an entire home in vintage space age, they got really excited." Originally, Wiedlin had planned on enlisting the Amors solely as purveyors of furniture and accessories to play off her own design scheme. But as she got to know the Jonamor Décor principals, the design firm suddenly found itself in charge of an entire decorating redo, from the installation of a space-cave bathroom complete with hanging decorative stalactites to the creation of an inner-planetary sleeping loft above an Asian-infused dressing room.

Miles tapped into Wiedlin's quirky interests, and soon thereafter touted a triumph on eBay that would start to set the tone for the rest of the project: a roll of silver-and-orange-swirled wallpaper that was used on the movie set of *Barbarella*. Jonona Amor installed the paper in the dining area as a background for a glass table with bulbous metallic-fabric upholstered chairs. Hanging above the set is a chrome, mid-'70s lighting fixture that infuses a jet-fueled spark. The orange splashes in the wallpaper established a continuous color story that was woven carefully throughout. It enlivens the space-aged metallics, the modern white furniture, and the clean walls of the industrial-looking area. And like any successful accent color, it enforces a planned outcome, even when it shows up molded around Wiedlin's favorite thrift find: a 1970s JVC Videosphere TV shaped like a space-mission helmet, ready to take Wiedlin off on her own intergalactic fantasy.

Dreamy Desires
Maison Rêve's Yasmine McGrane

Step over the threshold of this magical Victorian farmhouse nestled just off the road in Mill Valley, California, and you might wonder where all those scraped and peeling doors, poised just so behind a sofa or hanging on a wall, might lead. The admiration continues as you glide past a liberal sprinkling of light and airy antiques throughout, hover over lovingly bunched farmers' market flowers fashioned in canning jars and metal farm buckets, or dip your finger into an amber jar of honey that has been luring you from across the room since you set eyes on it. Why, there are actually people having fun in the next room. You can hear them. They sound as if they are having a few chuckles over a lighthearted game of Scrabble. And there really are birds chirping outside the window, so much so that you feel as if you're in one of those old Technicolor cartoons (except in this updated version, the colors are pale and subdued), and that one of those fine feathered friends just might, at any time, fly right through the front door, alight on your shoulder, and start tweeting a love song in your ear. Is this whole ethereal setting for real?

For Yasmine McGrane, who with her husband, David, created Maison Rêve as a design destination and a home for their young family, the total visual experience is transformed into a dreamy reality. Go ahead and ask McGrane about where those old doors behind a sofa might lead, and her

ABOVE LEFT A romantic Victorian bust atop a weathered dresser at the Alameda Point Antiques and Collectibles Faire.

BELOW LEFT Yasmine McGrane is always on the hunt for great doors, which she can usually find a use for. "I have so many doors in my warehouse, but I'm very particular about the ones I buy." More than often, the doors that she displays in her home and sells to clients are kept in the state that they were found in. "I love to just lean them up against the wall and let the color and character speak to me."

OPPOSITE McGrane took molding that she salvaged from an old Victorian home and turned it into a chalkboard frame, on which she posted the menu from a recent wine and cheese tasting that she hosted.

response may take a detour. Instead, she's more inclined to start tickling your creativity button, much the same way she does with clients in her quest to help them envision expressive uses for flea-market and thrift finds that she's convinced have much more life to give, even if they have been discarded.

At Maison Rêve, a turn-of-the-century, slotted wood mailbox turns into a showplace for clustered shapely letters of the alphabet; a French antique pie safe with mesh doors appears as spellbinding storage for fireplace logs; and a long, wooden device where hens used to perch and lay eggs now hangs on a living room wall displaying either rows of votives or flower buds in glass medicinal containers.

When it comes back to the doors that she voraciously collects, she can rattle a zillion uses for one of her many: a rustic table, an innovative room divider, a fanciful wall covering, a distinctive headboard, or an original mirror frame. Oh, and maybe you could just use it as it was conceived: as a door! But for her clients' sake, she purposely holds back. She guides their imaginations toward envisioning all the things they could do with the doors. "I like to use doors for decoration, because they can fill a large space with something architectural, and they make people think," says McGrane.

When she displays an item that's for sale at Maison Rêve, it is always tagged with information about its previous owner, if

ABOVE An inviting offer of wine and cheese makes shopping at Maison Rêve an event for all the senses.

OPPOSITE A sewing table with the machine removed and new drawer pulls turns into a quaint side table. Underneath, a fanciful feather tree that McGrane felt embodied the dreamy concept of Maison Rêve flutters next to a vintage lyre that she picked up on one of her first trips to Paris.

possible, and its origin. "It's not just about a pair of farm doors: it's the memory and the history that come with them."

With all the creativity that dwells inside Maison Rêve, the visitor might find it unfathomable to learn that McGrane once lived in a home that left her sad and unfulfilled as a creative person. "When I lived in the city, I was basically living out of a suitcase," says the Montreal native, who moved to San Francisco via Charlotte during the dot-com craze. "My apartment was just a place to store my things. I never had people over and I wasn't in a relationship. I felt like my whole life was totally out of balance."

As a way to take her overworked and underinspired mind away from all the crazy travel and stress of a job as a publicist and a living space void of personal décor, McGrane caught herself reaching back to her happiest childhood memories: sitting with her mother at the craft table; cutting, pasting, and drawing; and traveling with her throughout France perusing the world's most eclectic flea markets. There was something that spoke to her heart when she recalled the way her mother commandeered a flea market, opening creaky doors of nineteenth-century armoires and gingerly running her hands over aged and worn yet exquisite examples of upholstered furniture. Those past experiences stimulated McGrane's thinking. Maybe if she went to the local flea market in Charlotte she could lift her spirit and reinvigorate her soul. "So I got up really early one weekend morning, got into the car, and ended up at this huge flea market, where I stayed all day." One time a long pair of wood snowshoes tugged at her heart, conjuring up childhood images of a snowy day in Montreal. "I didn't quite know what to do with them, but I bought them because I just loved them," McGrane says. "Once I got home, I hung them on the wall, crisscrossed, and was so surprised at how much people loved them."

About another fantastic focal point in her apartment derived from yet another unlikely flea-market find, McGrane says, "I once took a pair of random shutters and put them on the front of a cabinet for storage in my little apartment, and it looked great!" That's when she seriously started pondering the possibilities of combining everything she loves to do-

ABOVE A glowing glass canning jar perches upon a wood rack once used by hens for egg laying.

OPPOSITE, LEFT Maison Rêve's prep room, where McGrane puts her farmers' market vegetables in neat, wood flea-market bins and her wine bottles in a riddling rack that she bought straight from the cellar of a restaurant in France.

making crafts, learning the history of old things, going to flea markets, and being ecologically mindful—and rolling it all up into a career. "Ultimately, I just decided that if I'm going to work this hard, then I want to be doing something that I really love," she says.

Now that McGrane has Maison Rêve, a place she calls an urban farmhouse, she never feels like she's working, even when she is. Her passion for flea markets has only intensified, qualifying her as a sought-after expert on this genre of shopping. "It's just so easy when you're driving down the road and see an estate sale and turn the steering wheel and go," she says. For McGrane, getting up at five on a Saturday morning, pulling on her trusted Wellies, and arriving first in line at the Alameda Point Antiques and Collectibles Faire is one of her all-time favorite things to do. In fact, McGrane has been known to rearrange travel plans just so she doesn't have to miss her favored flea market. "I love the hustle and bustle, seeing all the different things, and connecting with people," she says.

When McGrane hits the flea market, her main focus is finding antiques, but her technique applies to any flea-market or thrift-shopping experience. "It's easy," she explains. "I only buy what I love. Even if I'm buying for the store or for one of my clients, I only buy what I would have in my own home."

That philosophy applies to items of no "antique" value that simply speak to McGrane's tuned-in visual sensibility. She once bought a wagonload of shiny, blue Christmas ornaments for a few dollars, simply because she found them appealing. "I think I paid $70 for everything, when the wagon alone was worth $65," she says. "The vendor was happy because she had spent so much time collecting them, and she was pleased that the entire collection was going home together." Since McGrane paid cash, the vendor negotiated a deal. "Always take plenty of cash," McGrane recommends, especially since few vendors at flea markets are able to accept credit cards, and when they do, they are less likely to strike a bargain.

The time of day McGrane visits a flea market also affects the deal factor. "Either get there early, or get there late," McGrane says. At the

beginning of a flea market, she witnesses the broadest selection, but at the end, she'll be offered more bargains, since vendors would rather get rid of their wares than haul them all back home. Since she never knows how close to her car she'll be when she finds an unwieldy Victorian luster, yet another old door, or a set of French metal outdoor chairs, she always takes along her travel trolley so she can easily zip in and out of vendors' selling areas as well as cart any acquisitions.

McGrane buys only items that really speak to her heart, and doesn't let her shopping surge stray too far from Maison Rêve's aesthetic. She's not particularly interested in buying midcentury or retro-'70s furniture, avoids buying antique reproductions, and is always more inclined toward a purchase if it doesn't require a gigantic project to make it fit into her

ABOVE RIGHT Vintage French books are stacked on an old country table next to one of the twenty-six metal folding chairs she bought at a flea market. "They are great for when you have company,'" she says. "They just fold up and go out of the way. They also make a great side table, and are perfect for stacking towels and toiletry items in the bathroom."

design sensibility. "If something has good bones and just adding pretty knobs or a layer of paint or distressing the corners will make the difference, then it's a matter of having the time and desire, and it certainly doesn't take much time." With their walkie-talkies in hand ("You can't rely on mobile phone service at most flea markets I go to," she says), McGrane and her husband have turned their flea-marketing business into a lifestyle that for them is heaven sent.

"We love being at home now, and we love to entertain. We have guests and clients over all the time for wine and cheese tasting or for workshops on flower arranging, furniture recycling, or herb cooking," she says. And to think that not so long ago she never enjoyed having guests over. "Now it seems like nobody wants to leave!"

And at Maison Rêve, why would they?

RIGHT Even though Yasmin McGrane shies away from reproduction furniture, this piece spoke to her because of the authenticity, from the painted surface to the vintage hemp linen that went into its restoration. Upon it sits her prized flea-market Y, a wedding gift, and some of her favorite flea-market finds: vintage seed sacks.

OPPOSITE McGrane's Maison Rêve embodies the idea of an urban farmhouse. Here, a rabbit hutch becomes a decorative focal point underneath a distressed wooden table. To display fall foliage, McGrane gathered branches in a harvest pail. Another option she often uses for floral arrangements is one of the French enamel water pitchers that she keeps right by the door, close by a pair of her flea-marketing must-haves: her Wellie boots.

It Must Be Magic
Interior Designer James "Ford" Huniford

There is no public transportation to Fairyland, the magical island nestled among the Thousand Islands on the Saint Lawrence River, minutes away from Canada's border with New York State. The only practical way for guests to arrive at the peaceful 1920s home and boathouse of James "Ford" Huniford, founder of Huniford Design Studio, Ltd., and co-chair of the Dwellings furniture line, is via his boat at a mainland marina in Alexandria Bay. He's known for his opulent décor, and his well-known clients include the Newhouse family, the Rockefellers, Lauren and Richard Dupont, and Tina Turner.

On the way toward a spot of utter tranquility on Fairyland, bouncing against the crests in the water and taking in the still-warm spray cut by the boat, fall visitors notice geese bobbing up and down on the water, taking a break from their long flight south for the winter. And they marvel at the Boldt Castle, built by New York millionaire George C. Boldt, a hotel owner known for creating the signature Thousand Island dressing for the Waldorf-Astoria hotel.

Finally, after passing several smaller islands, some with lighthouses and others with homes, as well as the frequent scenic cruise or speed boat, guests alight at the dock on Fairyland Island, where Huniford has created a dreamy retreat on an estate once owned by the Schuler Company, which made Schuler Potato Chips. Huniford, a Syracuse native, selected the site for its ethereal calmness, its waterfront location, and its proximity to family.

Resting not far away from Huniford's stately vacation home, the two-room boathouse and captain's quarters that he completely redid is a fresh mix of Dwellings furniture, thrift-store discoveries, and flea-market

ABOVE LEFT Guests hang their totes above an old wicker sofa at Huniford's 1920s boathouse on the Saint Lawrence River.

BELOW LEFT The simplicity of the design in Huniford's boathouse on the Saint Lawrence River in upstate New York is what guests find relaxing to the mind and soul. Wood hoops hung on the wall add a decorative detail that is unobtrusive.

finds. The space is comfortable, uncompli-cated, and elegant, while making use of everyday objects that instantly put a guest at ease and make him or her want to linger for a while.

A thrift-store Georges Braque dove print sets a calming tone in a room filled with Huniford's finds. In the middle sits an orb made of pine cones found at a market in Belgium. Nearby is a pair of naturally crackled green fish-cutting tables that Huniford acquired from the Singer Mansion (of sewing machine fame) on nearby Dark Island. He has topped them with a variety of items that when listed, might not sound complementary: the remains of an old dartboard, a bamboo lamp, a metal pie cutter, and an antique wood minnow catcher, all found on flea-market escapades. How-ever, it's their weathered and aged finishes

ABOVE LEFT Huniford is known for incorporating found objects into his décor. Here, a bamboo lamp and a metal pie cutter sit atop a weathered fish-cutting table.

ABOVE A Georges Braque dove print from Housing Works oversees a room filled with Huniford's finds and his own furniture creations.

that make these objects go together seamlessly to invite curiosity and conversation. In the middle of the room is another thrift find: a low country table that's accented by a decorative gourd, some simple sunflowers, and a pair of tart cutters. The natural elements tie into the tone of the stone fireplace, the wood walls, and the sound of water lapping the dock just outside the door. The metal flea-market tart cutters, while man-made, maintain the symmetry of nature but could easily be mistaken for a nautical accessory. Void of TVs, video games, and stereo systems, the boathouse offers other diversions. Huniford's repurposed and unusual found accessories are all the entertainment required, contributing to the lazy, dazey oasis that exists only on Fairyland.

LEFT Huniford is known for incorporating unusual found objects that keep guests guessing what their real intended uses are. Here, the interior of a dartboard at left becomes an attractive decorative accessory along with a bamboo lamp and a wood minnow catcher.

OPPOSITE The dock is a great place to rock your cares away.

SIDE TABLE Once used to cut fish, a charming metal-topped table is preserved in its original peeling patina.

SIDE CHAIR A lacquered modernist plywood chair adds unexpected appeal among the other rustic details.

COFFEE TABLE A wood low-country table is topped with books and found objects.

DECORATIVE ACCESSORIES Leaned against the fireplace mantel, the display letter *H* pays tribute to the room's creator.

acknowledgments

The Find exists because of many talented people who so eagerly opened the doors to their homes, redecorated their interiors, threw theme parties, took me shopping, and shared their unique and endearing stories.

The Find is a testament to Housing Works' reputation for creating New York's premier thrift stores, where proceeds from sales go to eradicating homelessness and AIDS. Thank you to everyone at the organization for letting me rummage through your stores, for offering access to your experts, for opening up your files, and for providing a platform for me to explore the world of thrift and vintage. Matthew Bernardo, senior vice-president of Housing Works' business services, gave the green light to realize this book. A heartfelt thank-you goes out to you and to all of the store managers, employees, and volunteers who were patient during what seemed like an unending process. I also must thank artist Matthew Aquilone for his detailed insight into his early years of designing the iconic windows at Housing Works.

A special thank-you to a stellar group of designers who support the Housing Works mission through its annual benefit, "Design on a Dime." James "Ford" Huniford, Sharon Simonaire, Randall Beale, and Carl Lana's illustrative décors are symbolic of the amazing people who have made Housing Works a home-design destination. Thank you to every person featured in this book—some old friends and many new—who allowed me and my crew to document your inspiring creations.

I could never have achieved this book without the gorgeous photography of Jim Franco. Thank you for getting down on your knees in cat hair, for squeezing yourself *and* crew into teeny-tiny spaces, for taking a boat ride in the pouring rain, and, mostly, for seeing this project through to its finale. My deep gratitude also goes out to Bob Greenspan for capturing in photographs a magical journey to California and a side trip to Kansas City, resulting in imagery that I can honestly say is reflective of his amazingly creative eye.

Thank you, Doris Cooper, Clarkson Potter's editorial director, for your undying support of this project and for helping me make this book even better than I ever imagined. I also have to thank the entire Potter team for their expertise: Lauren Shakely, Marysarah Quinn, Lauren Monchik, Alexis Mentor, Mark McCauslin, and Angelin Borsics.

My literary agent, Robert Allen of Brands-to-Books, Inc., has always understood how important creating this book was to me and to the Housing Works mission. Thank you for guiding me through my first book project. An additional thank-you goes out to his business partner, Kathleen Spinelli, for letting me bend her ear during my wandering pursuit of *The Find*.

Ruth Handel has always been an unwavering source of encouragement and inspiration. I will always wake up at seven on a Saturday morning to go garage-saling with you in Santa Monica. You are a wonderful teacher and a cherished friend. Mark Ciolli, principal home decorator of Carl & Co., has so freely shared his encyclopedic knowledge of design and boosted my morale at every stage of this project. You are a true friend and a mentor.

I know I freaked out my mom and dad, Jerry and Deloris Williams, and my sister, Cheryl Bradley, when I told them I was going to dump a full-time magazine job to write a decorating book. You have always believed in me and have never stood in the way of my dreams, no matter how wacky they might seem. I love you dearly for those qualities.

Thank you to Beverly Smith, for understanding my need to create this book and for being a shining example of the kind of courage necessary to pursue the unknown. I could never have survived the journey without you, my Bevy. I am also grateful for Veli Ivanic, who patiently lived *The Find* with me every step of the way. Thank you for being with me to share this incredible adventure.

resources

Housing Works Thrift Shops

143 W. 17th St.
New York, NY 10011
718-838-5050

157 E. 23rd St.
New York, NY 10010
212-529-5955

306 Columbus Ave.
New York, NY 10023
212-579-7566

202 E. 77th St.
New York, NY 10021
212-772-8461

245 W. 10th St.
New York, NY 10014
212-352-1618

1730 Second Ave.
New York, NY 10128
212-722-8306

122 Montague St.
Brooklyn, NY 11201
718-237-0521

To donate or become a member of Housing Works, visit www.housingworks.org

benefit thrift stores

Brown Elephant Resale Shops
3651 N. Halsted St.
Chicago, IL 60613
773-549-5943

5404 N. Clark St.
Chicago, IL 60640
773-271-9382

1459 N. Milwaukee Ave.
Chicago, IL 60622
773-252-8801

217 Harrison St.
Oak Park, IL 60304
708-445-0612
www.howardbrown.org

Revivals Resale Marts
611 South Palm Canyon Dr.
Palm Springs, CA 92264
760-318-6491

73608 Highway 111
Palm Desert, CA 92260
760-346-8690

68100 Ramon Rd.
Cathedral City, CA 92234
760-328-1330

68-401 Highway 111
Cathedral City, CA 92234
760-969-5747
www.desertaidsproject.org

Out of the Closet
Multiple locations throughout California (LA, Berkeley, and San Francisco), and in Fort Lauderdale, Florida.
www.outofthecloset.org

thrift stores and vintage shops

Boomerang
1415 W. 39th St.
Kansas City, MO 64111
816-531-6111

Luticia Clementine's
206 N. Liberty St.
Independence, MO 64050
816-836-3822
www.luticiaclementines.com

Mission Road Antique Mall
4101 W. 83rd St.
Prairie Village, KS 66208
913-341-7577
www.missionroadantiquemall.com

R. E. Steele Antiques
74 Montauk Highway, No. 11
East Hampton, NY 11937
631-324-7812

Retro Inferno
1500 Grand Blvd.
Kansas City, MO 64108
816-842-4004
www.retroinferno.com

Retropia
1443 N. Highland
Hollywood, CA 90028
323-871-4000
www.retropia.net

River Market Antique Mall
115 W. Fifth St.
Kansas City, MO 64105
816-221-0220
www.rivermarketantiquemall.com

Two Jakes
320 Wythe Ave.
Brooklyn, NY 11211
718-782-7780
www.twojakes.com

flea markets

**Alameda Point Antiques and
Collectibles Faire**
Alameda, CA 94501
510-522-7500
www.antiquesbybay.com

Alemany Flea Market
100 Alemany Blvd.
San Francisco, CA 94110
415-647-2043

**Brimfield Antique and Flea
Market Show**
Brimfield, MA 01010
www.brimfield.com

Brooklyn Flea
Bishop Loughlin Memorial High
School
357 Clermont Ave.
Brooklyn, NY 11238
www.brooklynflea.com

Gammel Strand Flea Market
Copenhagen, Denmark
+45-35-26-18-21

New York City Flea Markets
As of press time, the future of
Manhattan's much-heralded flea
markets is uncertain. For updates, visit
www.hellskitchenfleamarket.com

Porte de Vanves Flea Market
Paris, France
www.pucesdeparis-portedevanves.com

Rose Bowl Flea Market
1001 Rose Bowl Dr.
Pasadena, CA 91103
323-560-7469
www.rgcshows.com

**Santa Monica Airport Outdoor
Antique & Collectible Market**
Airport Ave. off of Bundy
Los Angeles, CA 90405
www.santamonicaairportantique
market.com

**Saint-Ouen Flea Market
(Porte de Clignancourt)**
Paris, France
www.parispuces.com

design resources

Apartment Therapy
www.apartmenttherapy.com

Beale-Lana Interior Design
300 E. 57th St.
New York, NY 10022
212-813-2213
www.beale-lana.com

Carl & Co. Interior Design
187 Chrystie St., Suite 8
New York, NY 10002
www.carlandco.com

Carl Martinez Hardware
83 Canal St.
New York, NY 10002
212-941-8142
www.carlmartinezhardware.com

**David Jimenez, Visual
Merchandising Professional**
www.djimenez.com

Doyle Auctions
175 E. 87th St.
New York, NY 10128
212-427-4141
www.doylenewyork.com

Dwellings
800-95-DECOR
www.dwellingshome.com

Huniford Design Studio, Ltd.
800-490-0309
www.huniford.com

Joe Maer, Prop Stylist
www.joemaer.com

John Derian Company
6 E. Second St.
New York, NY 10003
212-677-3917

John Derian Dry Goods
10 E. Second St.
New York, NY 10003
212-677-8408
www.johnderian.com

John Esty Custom Framing
44 Greenwich Ave.
New York, NY 10011
212-691-3753

Jonamor Décor
323-428-3782
www.jonamordecor.com

Jordan Cappella Collection, LLC
310-625-0822
www.jordancappella.com

Maison Rêve
101 Throckmorton Ave.
Mill Valley, CA 94941
415-383-9700
www.maisonreve.com

Michelle Rago, Ltd.
150 W. 25th St., Suite 501
New York, NY 10001
212-736-0195
www.michelleragoltd.com

Office of Mobile Design
1725 Abbott Kinney Blvd.
Venice, CA 90291
310-439-1129
www.designmobile.com

Osmundo Echevarria & Associates
2107 Borden Ave.
Long Island City, NY 11101
718-707-9610

Palm Springs Modern Committee
www.psmodcom.com

Peter Frank, Set Designer and Prop Stylist
www.peterfrank.com

Serv ce Station
2440 A Route 28
Glenford, NY 12433
845-657-9788
www.servcestation.com

Sharon Simonaire Interior Design
212-242-1824
www.sharonsimonaire.com

Skellramics
11024 Balboa Blvd., #629
Granada Hills, CA 91344
818-360-6599
www.skellramics.com

Turquoise Interior Design
633 Palms Blvd.
Venice, CA 90291
310-578-1722
www.turquoise-la.com

other featured resources

Alison Attenborough, Food Stylist
www.alisonattenborough.com

Beqaj Real Estate
302 West Walk
Saltaire, NY 11706
631-583-0350
www.beqajrealestate.com

Fred Flare, Lifestyle Retailer
www.fredflare.com

Jamie Kimm, Food Consultant
www.jamiekimm.com

John Bartlett, Fashion Designer
143 Seventh Ave.
New York, NY 10014
212-633-6867
www.johnbartlettny.com

Patch NYC, Fashion Designers
www.patchnyc.com

featured photographers

Jim Franco
www.jimfranco.com

Bob Greenspan
www.bobgreenspan.com

Anna Moller
www.annamoller.net

index

about the author and photographers

STAN WILLIAMS is a New York–based lifestyle journalist. He has written for *Maxim, Latina,* and *American Express Executive Travel,* among other publications. A native of Independence, Missouri, and a graduate of the University of Missouri–Columbia Journalism School, Williams documents his favorite finds on www.theobjectofmydesire.com.

JIM FRANCO is a lifestyle and interiors photographer whose client list includes Williams-Sonoma and Pottery Barn, *Condé Nast Traveler UK, Domino, Real Simple,* Habitat Hotels, Aqua Hotel Group, and *Lexus* magazine. He was the photo editor at *Rolling Stone* and *Travel + Leisure.*

BOB GREENSPAN is an architecture and design photographer. He is a frequent contributor to *Better Homes & Gardens.*